The LOST VILLAGES

The
LOST VILLAGES

In Search of
Britain's Vanished Communities

Henry Buckton

I.B. TAURIS
LONDON · NEW YORK

Published in 2008 by I.B.Tauris & Co Ltd
6 Salem Road, London W2 4BU
175 Fifth Avenue, New York NY 10010
www.ibtauris.com

In the United States of America and Canada distributed
by Palgrave Macmillan, a division of St. Martin's Press,
175 Fifth Avenue, New York NY 10010

ISBN: 978 1 84511 671 2

A full CIP record for this book is available from the British Library
A full CIP record is available from the Library of Congress
Library of Congress Catalog Card Number: available

Design and typesetting by E&P Design, Bath
Printed and bound in Great Britain by TJ International Ltd,
Padstow, Cornwall

CONTENTS

The LOST VILLAGES

Village chapter numbers
and Ordnance Survey references:

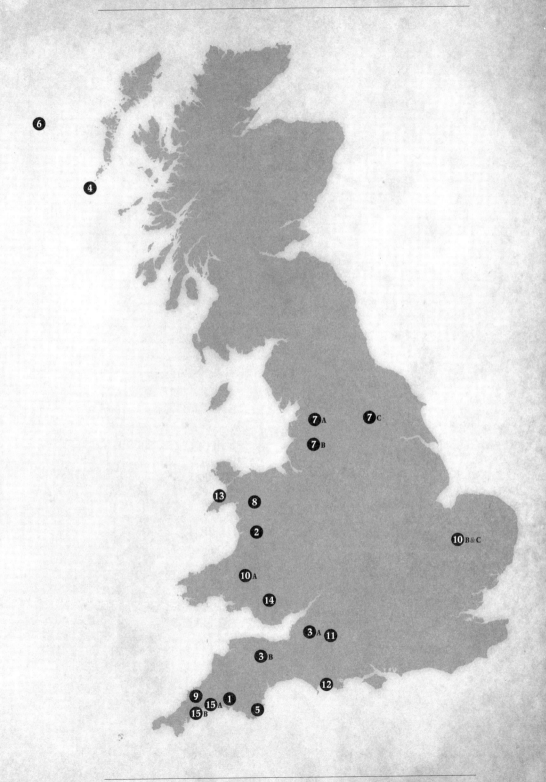

INTRODUCTION

All over Britain you can find the remains of villages that were once busy and full of life, but which now lie silent and still. Their dates vary from the ancient to the relatively modern. At Grimspound on Dartmoor, for example, you find a Bronze Age village, while little more than half a mile down the lane towards Widecombe in the Moor you will discover the remains of Challacombe – a medieval village with its ruined longhouse and system of strip lynchets still visible on the hillside. Half a mile to the west lies evidence of a major Victorian mining site that once employed 150 people in a mass of buildings, diggings and large waterwheels – all now gone. None of these settlements happened haphazardly; they were built at these locations for good reasons, and disappeared for others.

These villages are now referred to as 'lost villages' or some-times 'ghost villages', and there are an estimated 3,000 of them. Many date from pre, or medieval history and the reasons for their disappearance are varied. Some were affected by natural causes, such as changing climate, coastal erosion, flooding, or the changing course of a river.

Often communities were deliberately displaced or forced to move because of the changing economy. In the fourteenth century, large areas of Scotland were cleared because the landowners had replaced arable farming with livestock. There was more money to be made from wool and meat than there was from crop production, and fewer labourers were needed. This situation led to mass emigration. Similarly, as a consequence of the famine in Ireland during the mid-nineteenth century, many people had no alternative but to emigrate if their families were to survive. In both of these instances, many villages, hamlets and farms were left abandoned as people sought to improve their lives in foreign lands.

Then, of course, there were villages built around natural resources, where for example quarrying or mining took place. When the resource ran out the village became unsustainable, and the people had to move to find work. The same principle often applied in agricultural villages, as over the years improved technology and mechanisation meant that fewer jobs were available on the land.

Famously, the bubonic plague in 1348 caused many villages to change location. When you discover an isolated church in a rural area with no other buildings around it, the local people sometimes claim the church stands alone because of the 'Black Death'. Other than the church, most buildings were made of wood and when the plague ravaged the village, the entire settlement was burnt to the ground and rebuilt in another location. How much of this is truth, and how much myth, is difficult to ascertain. Bearing in mind that roughly half the population of the country died during this terrible period, the plague probably did contribute to the eradication of some entire communities. But the reasons why churches sometimes stand in isolation might reflect any one of the above scenarios.

In this book we study villages that met their end during the twentieth century, the most diverse period in history. Because of this diversity, there are many different factors contributing to the end of communities that in some instances had existed for a thousand years. Also, because it is still relatively recent in our past, there are people alive who can either remember living in these communities or are descended from those who did. Through photographs and memories we can actually put names, faces and characters to the people who were displaced. Standing on the site of a remote ancient settlement on Dartmoor, it is hard to have any real affinity with the people who lived there. But when we come across an overgrown village that disappeared less than 100 years ago, there is a greater sense of sadness for their loss. After all, these people were very like us: they spoke the same language; dressed in a similar fashion; they went to school; found jobs locally; married and had children; they took part in the life of the village, its clubs, sports and festivals.

As well as studying the villages themselves, this book is an exercise in social history – an examination of how our near ancestors lived during the early part of the twentieth century. In some ways, these lost villages also represent a lost lifestyle, a way of life trapped in time. Even 50 years ago, the lives of everyday people – our parents, grandparents, and great grandparents – were very different from those that we live today.

The Bessie Belle and Matilda taking scrap away from Morwellham Quay in 1903

Photograph courtesy of Morwellham and Tamar Valley Trust

1

A LOST VILLAGE LIVES AGAIN

At the start of the twentieth century Britain was changing rapidly and some villages disappeared as a result of these changes. Even though the new century would bring unimaginable advances in science and technology, Britain's dominant status in the world was on the wane. The Victorian age made Britain 'Great'. It was a time of great engineers and innovators, when the industrial revolution brought commerce to every corner of the kingdom. By 1851, British factories and engineering works were at their height of productivity, a situation reflected in the Great Exhibition at Crystal Palace opened by Queen Victoria on 1 May. This historic event was a celebration of Britain's industrial prowess.

Our journey begins in a wooded valley along the River Tamar, the border between Devon and Cornwall, in a quiet rural backwater a few miles from Tavistock. This picturesque country setting might appear out of place when discussing the industrial revolution. However, in the 1860s, Morwellham Quay was the busiest inland port in the west of England. Yet just 100 years later during the 1960s, the cottages had become ivy covered ruins, the quays silted up, and the docks abandoned.

Thousands of tourists visit Morwellham Quay each year, so you might think it is an unusual place to begin a tour of Britain's ghost villages: indeed, the village was never totally abandoned and several cottages have seen continuous occupation. But in one respect it is probably an ideal place to begin our journey if we are to understand the way people lived in Britain 100 years ago, as well as some of the reasons why several communities disappeared at the turn of the twentieth century. Also, if you had been fortunate enough to visit Morwellham Quay before the 1970s, you would have observed a very different scene from that of today. At that time, other than a handful of surviving houses that were still being lived in, it was exactly what you would have expected from a ghost village: the school had closed, the workers had moved away, and most of the buildings were abandoned, forgotten and ruined.

In 1969, the Morwellham and Tamar Valley Trust began its work at Morwellham Quay, commissioning teams of archaeologists, surveyors and historians to research the mines and village, and to begin the painstaking work of restoring these to their former glory, thus preserving part of Britain's industrial heritage for future generations.

The village has now been restored to how it would have appeared in the 1860s when around 300 people lived there, with many more walking in daily from nearby villages and hamlets to work on the quays. At some of the restored cottages you are afforded an insight into how people lived at the time, but very little would have changed domestically by the turn of the century. You can see the lamps that were used to light the home; the sculleries where women spent all day on a Monday washing the clothes in the copper before rinsing them in a bucket and pressing them through a mangle; the open fires on which the poorer people cooked and the ranges used by the more affluent; the bath tubs in which they bathed; and the outside lavatories that offered little more than a hole in a wooden shelf with a bucket beneath. When you read some of the personal accounts later in the book you will observe that conditions at some of the villages we visit had changed very little by the middle of the twentieth century.

But how had this small riverside village come to such prominence, only to slide once again into obscurity? Morwellham Quay was originally established by the Benedictine monks who had founded Tavistock Abbey in 974 AD. So it is quite probable that the original settlement pre-dates the Norman Conquest. At Morwellham Quay the monks found that a stream joining the River Tamar was a useful place for landing a boat. By navigating the river to this point, they were able to establish a quayside from which boats could bring supplies for the abbey and, just as importantly, export the woolen cloth that was being produced at Tavistock on which the abbey's wealth depended.

After the dissolution of the monasteries in the 1530s, the land passed to the Russell family, who would later become the Dukes of Bedford. But by now the real value of the village was becoming evident. The whole area was rich with minerals and metallic ores and successive mining booms transformed the site into a bustling inland port. The surroundings brimmed with tin, silver ore, lead ore, arsenic and copper, some of which was brought to the quaysides by packhorses toiling across the hills from Dartmoor.

At the time of Elizabeth I copper was in great demand for the manufacture of canons and other items of ordnance, a demand which continued right through to the early nineteenth century when Britain was at war with Napoleon. Copper was not only used in the manufacture of weapons but for a wide variety of things – from machines, engines, boilers, pots and pans to coins and the fittings of carriages and trains. It was even pressed into sheets to plate the bottom of ships. Therefore, the lodes in the Tamar Valley set the scene for a mining boom that would last at various levels of intensity until 1900.

As the activity in the Tamar Valley steadily intensified, the roads were still very basic and the trains of packhorses bringing the ore would make them muddy and hazardous. So, as early as 1803, a brilliant mining engineer named John Taylor began work on the Tavistock Canal, linking Morwellham Quay to the town four miles away, and from there the mines of western Dartmoor. The packhorses would bring their loads from the mines to Tavistock, from where iron barges would ferry them down to the port, returning with lime, coal and timber. However, building a canal in such hilly terrain was no simple task, so Taylor designed it with a gentle decline. This meant that although barges were able to come down to Morwellham Quay from Tavistock on the current, the return journey necessitated the use of poles to push them through a tunnel that was one and a half miles long, before being hitched to ponies for the remaining haul into town.

In 1844, it was discovered that Morwellham itself had its own important resource, as a massive lode of copper ore passed through the hillside close to the port. The resulting mines, run by the Devonshire Great Consolidated Mining Company, would produce somewhere in the region of 700,000 tonnes of copper ore and 72,000 tonnes of arsenic during a 60-year period. At the height of its activity, this complex of five mines covering an area of 167 acres was served by a comprehensive transport system, which included the Tavistock Canal and three separate railways, two of which were built on inclined lines. During this period the valley would prove to be Europe's leading source of copper, and more shipping navigated the River Tamar than the Mersey. It became so busy that at several places along its banks there was a series of continuous quays: not only at Morwellham but at places like Newquay and Gawton. At some places along the quiet lanes today you can still see stones inscribed with the words 'to the quays'. One of these can be found near the old tollhouse at Rock, while another situated along the road to Bere Alston points to Gawton Quay.

In the restored village school room there is a series of long benches that most people will recognise from their school days as being called forms. Every child was taught in the same room – no matter what their age. So in order to distinguish between them, the children in their first year would sit on the front bench, known as the first form; the second year pupils would sit on the second form and so on. There are, however, very few forms in the school room, because many children born to mining families before the Education Acts of 1876 left school and began work at around eight years of age.

The realisation that such young children were engaged in so dangerous and frightening an occupation illustrates the point that, for most people at Morwellham, life was more about survival than enjoyment. It was a hard, cruel existence, a continual struggle, and each job on offer presented its own dangers.

Without doubt the most dangerous job was that of the copper miners themselves, who worked in cramped and dirty conditions. First there were dangers posed by the mine, which included roof falls and flooding. Some of the mines went deep underground, even going beneath the river, and flooding could happen almost without warning. The water was polluted due to unsanitary conditions, often spreading viral diseases. To combat this, a large waterwheel – similar to those used at mills – was installed in the mine to pump water out of the tunnels. Long ladders would have to be negotiated while carrying heavy equipment, resulting in regular falls. Prolonged work in poorly lit conditions led to many sight defects, in severe cases even blindness. Others were blinded by flying rock fragments. Apparently an early form of Braille was developed in the nearby mining community of Bere Alston. The noise of underground explosions and drilling caused deafness. And perhaps worst of all was the dusty atmosphere, which when breathed into the lungs caused extreme respiratory problems, even premature death. So all in all, mines of any description were not very pleasant places in which to work.

To extract copper, the early miners would heat the rock and then pour cold water over the heated surface, causing the rock to crack and making it easier to hammer out the ore. The process was improved with the arrival of gunpowder, which would be packed into natural cracks in the rock or into cavities specially carved out for the purpose. However, these explosions proved to be very dangerous, often causing cave-ins and generating massive amounts of dust. Fuses made from straw or quills combined with small amounts of gunpowder were used to trigger these explosions. As one can imagine they were extremely unreliable and premature explosions caused many deaths. The safety fuse of 1831, which was a length of cord filled with gunpowder, improved things greatly.

During the 1860s, a compressed air drill operated by two people was introduced. An adult miner would do the drilling, while one of the younger boys, perhaps even one of the eight-years-olds, would hold the drill steady. While drills such as these certainly improved productivity – and the wealth of the mine owners – they had terrible consequences on the health of their operators. Standing next to the drill and holding it for hours on end caused many of the boys to be profoundly deaf by the age of 20. The drill would also cause clouds of thick, choking dust. Neither the man nor the lad would be likely to live beyond 40, and because of this the air drill was nicknamed the 'Widow Maker'.

Miners would remain underground for their entire working day (often for 10 or 12 hours) and during the winter months would only see sunlight once a week – on Sunday. Lunch at the mines of western Devon, similar to those of Cornwall, would have been a pasty. Within the pastry case, a traditional miner's pasty would have meat and vegetables in one end and fruit or jam in the other, thus presenting a two course meal. The miner's wife or mother would mark the crust with his initials, so that he would know which end was which at lunchtime. These pasties were eaten in the dim light whilst sitting on a rock with filthy hands, as there were no washing facilities below ground. Often the thick pastry rim, contaminated by the miner's dirty hands, would be thrown away at the end of the meal.

Things were marginally better for those working on the surface, many of whom were young girls and women known as bal maidens. The word 'bal' derives from an old Cornish word for mine, and the maidens were often as young as eight or nine. Normally, married women did not work at the mines, so the workforce comprised of young unmarried women and widows. Their job was to dress the ore, which involved separating the metal from rocks that had been brought up to the surface from the mine.

At different sites along the Tamar, processes varied depending on the metal being extracted, but as a general rule the work of the bal maidens fell into one of three categories: sorting, washing and transporting; mechanical breaking; and the separation of finer ores by sedimentation techniques. The various jobs were allocated according to age but they were all physically demanding and required high levels of skill and strength.

The ore would first be washed and sorted by the very youngest girls, according to its weight and appearance. Young teenagers would then sieve the rock through boxes called jigs that would separate out the medium sized portions of copper ore. The older females would do the backbreaking work of spalling, cobbing and bucking. All three of these involved the use of hammers to break up the rock. During spalling, with an aptly named spalling hammer, the rock would be broken into fist sized pieces; a cobbing hammer would break it into marble sized chunks; and bucking would involve grinding the smallest pieces into almost powder form.

Bal maidens had a distinctive dress style, wearing steel tipped shoes or clogs and a bonnet known as a gook that covered much of their face and shoulders. This was their only protection against flying shards or the winter weather through which they continued to toil. They also wore an apron called a towser and those that could afford them would have two. One was worn while walking to and from the mines to try and look decent, while the other was put on for working at the dressing floors. This sounds a very drab uniform but it shows that against a background of adversity they took pride in their appearance. There is also evidence to suggest that bal maidens could be quite gay and colourful. When Queen Victoria visited the Duke of Bedford at Endsleigh, his summer retreat in 1856, she arrived at Morwellham Quay by paddle steamer from Plymouth and continued her journey by coach along the Duke's riverside drive, which can still be seen in part today. The bal maidens gathered at the quay to greet the Queen, wearing bonnets festooned with different coloured ribbons. Victoria was so moved by the sight that she reputedly asked for some of the ribbons as a keepsake.

Both miners and bal maidens were poorly paid. At the end of the nineteenth century a miner would earn around 15 shillings a

Morwellham Quay photographed in 1906, with the quays and docks deserted

Photograph courtesy of Morwellham and Tamar Valley Trust

Village children playing on Morwellham's deserted Higher Copper Quay around 1914

Photograph courtesy of Morwellham and Tamar Valley Trust

This photograph from an unknown mine provides a good illustration of the clothes worn by bal maidens and other workers

Photograph courtesy of Morwellham and Tamar Valley Trust

week and a bal maiden roughly six or seven. Everyone worked from Monday to Saturday lunchtime, and the only holidays were Christmas Day, Good Friday, and possibly the parish feast day. On Midsummer's Day the mines were spring-cleaned and the work-force was permitted to leave early. They were also given money to spend at the Midsummer Fair. This presumably was considered as a bonus but for men it usually amounted to around 12 pence, and for the women about six pence.

Many people worked on the quayside, loading copper ore onto the boats that would ferry it down the river towards Plymouth. From the mine area to the quay, the ore was loaded onto trucks that were pushed by hand on an inclined railway. At the quay, the trucks were unhitched and taken to a siding, from where their cargo would be unloaded by hand and stacked in piles ready for the next boat. These workers were paid one penny for every tonne they loaded and unloaded on the quay, and made an estimated 10 shillings a week – not as much as the miners but certainly more than the bal maidens and other surface workers.

One of the most important men in the village was the assayer, who managed the quayside. One aspect of his job was to test ore samples to ascertain the quality of the copper. He did this in a laboratory where, after crushing the ore into powder and adding various chemicals, it was burnt to see how much metal would remain. From this he was able to put a price on the ore as it stacked up on the quayside. At the height of productivity every available space at the quays was crammed with copper ore awaiting shipment, and those at neighbouring places such as Newquay and Gawton. The assayer worked long hours, both testing the ore and managing the quayside, for which he received around £4 a week. Compared to miners and bal maidens, this was a huge amount of money, so he was able to live in some style. He would have been well-educated, and also had assistant samplers that were paid around £1 a week: such jobs were highly prized in a mining community.

At Morwellham Quay, the reconstructed cottages offer stark comparisons between the relative luxury of the assayer and the squalid conditions in which the miners lived. The assayer's house had a large kitchen, which doubled up as an office; a parlour; two bedrooms; and a scullery. The parlour was rarely used other than for entertaining guests, so the kitchen with its table and chairs was the hub of household activity. For cooking, the large fireplace had an integrated oven or 'range'. The room would also have a

Welsh dresser displaying decorative china and many utensils that miners could never afford, such as a skimmer for making cream, a potato masher and a marmalade slicer, used to cut up fruit. There would also have been a meat press for tenderising different joints, as well as a great variety of pots, pans, jars and metal cutlery. In the scullery would be the copper for boiling the clothes, the poshy tub and long handled posser used to agitate all the washing, a mangle, and several flat irons.

Both bedrooms in the assayer's house were upstairs and had comfortable beds with sheets and blankets for all the family. The miner's cottage normally had a bed for the husband and wife, but the rest of the family, which included numerous children and sometimes even grandparents and lodgers, would sleep on sacking on the floor. The cottage usually comprised of three small downstairs rooms in which a dozen or more people would often live. There was a small fireplace in the living room on which a metal rack was used for cooking. The family might own a metal kettle to boil water and a tin in which to cook their diet of stodgy food, mainly potatoes and turnips. Most families reared a pig, which was kept in a sty at the back of the house behind the outside lavatories until it was ready for butchering. With so many people in a confined space, and with non-flushing toilets and pigs near the back door, the smell was very unpleasant in summer, and flies would have been a serious problem.

But by 1900, the massive lode of copper ore at Morewellham was all but exhausted and the mines were systematically closing down. The pumps of the Devonshire Great Consolidated Mining Company finally stopped working in 1901. The now extensive rail network linking Tavistock to every part of Britain meant there was little point in using either the canal or the River Tamar to transport what little ore remained. Remnants of the mining industry around Tavistock and Dartmoor survived until the 1920s, but Morwellham Quay had served its purpose and the population began to move away.

As well as the school, the village had two chapels, one Wesleyan and the other United Methodist Free Church. There were also large lime kilns, a smithy, hotel, cooperage, wainright, and shop – all the trappings of a successful community. The Duke of Bedford paid for the building of many of the cottages himself to cater for the growing population, including some of those which are now open to the public. But by the time of the First World War, the village

Jane Martin's slate-hung shop photographed about 1914, which sold cream teas to day-trippers who visited Morwellham Quay by paddle-steamer from Plymouth

Photograph courtesy of Morwellham and Tamar Valley Trust

This photograph taken in 1986 shows the limeburner's cottage with its restoration nearing completion. This was one of several ruined buildings at Morwellham Quay that have been restored for future generations to understand how their ancestors lived

Photograph courtesy of Morwellham and Tamar Valley Trust

was already practically deserted and the majority of properties had fallen into disrepair.

Morwellham Quay was one of a series of forgotten villages and hamlets situated along both banks of the River Tamar, such as Newquay, Gawton, Calstock, Halton Quay, and Weir Quay, some of which went into terminal decline. So its reconstruction could be considered representative of several lost communities from all over west Devon and east Cornwall. Throughout its history, even during its busiest period in the 1860s, industry and agriculture worked side by side in the Tamar Valley. Agriculture ultimately prevailed and, as the nineteenth century ended and the twentieth century began, the area had reverted from a hectic centre of Victorian industrialisation back to the peaceful rural valley that existed before the arrival of the Benedictine monks. In such a tranquil and picturesque setting, it is now hard to imagine the frantic activity and the thousands of people who had lived and worked here: thriving communities now resigned to the pages of history.

2

FROM RICHES
TO RAGS

The virtual abandonment of thriving communities, as a result of the closure of local mines around the turn of the twentieth century, was certainly not unique to the Tamar Valley. Some communities, although suffering economic hardship and a degree of population loss as people moved to find alternative employment, survived by replacing mining with other industrial enterprises. Others survived because their geographical location enabled the inhabitants to commute to neighbouring settlements in order to find work.

In mid-Wales, on a remote road between Machynlleth and Llanidloes, in a windswept wilderness of mountains and moorland, you will still find a few houses collectively known as Dylife. Similar to Morwellham Quay, these houses are the remnants of a once important mining community, which was abandoned around 100 years ago. It evolved over the centuries from a group of scattered farmsteads into a bustling village of the Victorian age supporting around 1,000 souls, complete with parish church, post office, school and smithy. At one time the excavations here were regarded as the glory of the Montgomeryshire mines until their importance was eclipsed by those at Van, to the south-east. But unlike numerous other mining villages, it was Dylife's very remoteness that ushered its downfall, because when the mines closed it was too distant from any other sources of employment to make it sustainable.

Lead mining at Dylife had begun as early as the Roman occupation. At Pen y Crogben, a stone's throw to the south, there was a Roman road and fortlet. In the surrounding area there is evidence to suggest that both copper and lead ore were being mined as far back as the Bronze Age. Before its dramatic growth in the nineteenth century, Dylife was most famous – or perhaps

Dylife photographed in the late nineteenth century, with Rhod Goch at the centre and miners' cottages seen in the distance

Photograph courtesy of Powysland Museum

The remains of Siôn Jones, now on display in St Fagans National History Museum, near Cardiff

Photograph courtesy of Stephen Fisk

infamous – for the brutal murders of three people: a woman and her two children. During the early eighteenth century, people were already beginning to move into the area in search of employment. One such person was a blacksmith from Ystumtuen in Cardiganshire, named Siôn Jones, who arrived in Dylife around 1719, leaving his wife and children at home. Soon after his arrival he began to have an affair with a local woman, a maid at Llwyn y Gog, a short distance away, who he subsequently married.

Several weeks later his wife paid him an unexpected visit, bringing his two children on foot to spend a few days with him. The two areas were joined by rough tracks skirting the mountain of Plynlimon, which provides the sources of both the rivers Wye and Severn. On their return journey, Jones murdered them and threw their bodies down a disused mineshaft at Dyfngwm, a short way to the south-west.

Some time later, three workmen who had been sent to Dyfngwm to retrieve some of the old timbers that were going to waste in the mineshaft made the gruesome discovery of the three bodies. Siôn Jones was arrested and put on trial for the murder of his wife and children. and, having been found guilty he was ordered – as the village blacksmith – to make his own hanging frame. On the day of his execution he was taken to Pen y Crogben, the site of the old Roman fortlet where, with the frame suspended from a gallows, he was obliged to sit on the back of a horse until the animal was made to move forward. In 1938, the landowner Will Richards, himself an ex-miner, unearthed part of an iron frame and a skull. These are now on display at St Fagans National History Museum, near Cardiff, where the skull is claimed to be that of the murderous Siôn Jones.

The modern history of Dylife really begins around 1800, at which time most of the land in the area was owned by Sir Watkin Williams-Wynn, who was reputed to own so much of Wales that he could travel to Machynlleth from his home in Wrexham without leaving his own property. In 1814, he leased the land at Dylife to Hugh Williams and John Pughe, two men from Machynlleth who had latterly managed the mines.

Although these two individuals were largely responsible for the surging success of these mining operations, they had an uneasy working relationship. It had taken them five years to negotiate the terms of the lease. Stephen Fisk, who has researched the village explains:

The signing of the lease was delayed because they failed to produce satisfactory financial accounts and articles of partnership that would govern their working relationship. They obtained the lease in 1814, and they and their successors continued to operate the mines until the 1850s. But through- out this period financial management continued to be unsatisfactory, and there were repeated difficulties in relations between the two lease holders. When there was a need to purchase new equipment, for example, both men would pay half the cost. Employees were paid twice a week, on separate days, receiving half their wages from Williams and half from Pughe. There was resentment between the two men, with Williams taking the view that Pughe was devoting much less time and energy to the management of the mines than he was.

Disagreements aside, the mines were extremely profitable and, as well as lead, they yielded significant quantities of copper, zinc and silver. New shafts were dug and machinery was brought in to assist with pumping, drawing, crushing the ore, and extracting the lead. Much of this machinery was powered by a series of massive waterwheels: most spectacularly Rhod Goch, or the Red Wheel. Erected in 1851, it had a diameter of 63 feet and a width of three and a half feet. It was unquestionably one of the largest waterwheels in Britain at the time, possibly second only to the Lady Isabella on the Isle of Man. But not all of this machinery was powered by water: for instance, a blowing machine, which aided ventilation, was operated by young lads turning a handle. So the overall operation was a mixture of new and old technologies, mechanisation and manpower. Headstones in the churchyard indicated that many of Dylife's male population died between the ages of 36 and 40, but similar to the Tamar Valley, children as young as eight would have been employed in various roles.

Where the mining operation at Dylife did lose some of its profitability was in the transportation of the lead ore to the smelters, at places like Bristol, Chester and Liverpool. Morwellham Quay was ideally placed and able to use the River Tamar as its transport artery, but Dylife sat in the remote mountains of mid-Wales. The ore therefore had to be transported across rough mountain tracks to the port of Derwenlas, near the mouth of the River Dyfi, some 12 miles away. Here it was loaded on to ships for delivery to the smelters.

In order to transport the ore to Derwenlas, Williams and Pughe employed local farmers to use their horse drawn carts. Even this caused problems, as the roads were narrow and winding, and in the droving season they would encounter herds of cattle and flocks of sheep coming in the opposite direction. The drovers would utilise mountain passes that took them through Dylife and on towards mid-Wales, and England beyond. They would stay overnight at the Drop Inn, which was situated at the western end of the village, and they would have shoes put on the cattle at Rhyd y Porthmyn farm, before continuing their journey. At such times the local farmers would no doubt have mixed loyalties, as they were able to make money from both the drovers and the mining company.

In 1852, an article in the *Mining Journal* noted that celebrations were held at Dylife for the wedding of the landowner, the current Sir Watkin Williams-Wynn, at which time around 300 people lived in the village. On 28 April, all employees of the mining company were invited to a party to celebrate the occasion and, according to the article, they were supplied with tea, coffee and cold meat. It was reported that the mountain of Plynlimon, overlooking the scene, resounded with hilarity and song, despite the absence of any alcohol.

Wedding celebrations aside, these were not particularly happy times for Dylife, as the relationship between Williams and Pughe continued to decline. But the fortunes of the village were soon to take an upturn after the men agreed that their best solution was to sell the mines. At this point, Richard Cobden appears on the scene, one of Britain's most eminent politicians and the man who had famously led the opposition to the Corn Laws. Cobden, who was married to the youngest daughter of Hugh Williams, played a major part in the sale of the mines and the creation of a new company to administer them. In partnership with another senior politician, John Bright, Cobden persuaded a group of Manchester businessmen to buy shares in the new company, and the Dylife Mining Company Limited was registered on 7 July 1858, under the chairmanship of Bright himself.

All of this was good news for both the village and the mines. Stephen Fisk notes that:

> *Within a few years the new company had done a great deal to develop the operation of the mines. New shafts were dug vertically so that cages could be installed to lower and raise the*

miners and to bring up the wagons containing ore. In other lead mines at that time miners would descend at an angle by ladder, and the ore was still being drawn up in large buckets known as kibbles. Another waterwheel was put in place to provide power to a system of metal ropes that transported ore over a mile from two mine shafts to the dressing floors. Changing rooms were provided, Dylife being the only mine in mid-Wales, north Wales, or Shropshire to have such a facility.

Transportation remained the company's only major concern. However, in 1864, the problem of getting ore quickly and efficiently to the smelters was resolved when the railway arrived at the village of Llanbrynmair on the line that joined Aberystwyth to Shrewsbury. Llanbrynmair was only eight miles from Dylife and the road to it was much better than the mountain track to Derwenlas. For most of its length it also followed a gentle downward slope.

By now the village had established a true sense of community. It was no longer regarded as just a place where outsiders came to secure employment. It now had its own identity, where much of the population could trace their ancestors back several generations – and the village was still growing.

Welsh mining communities were very religious and a diversity of denominations were catered for by several chapels. An Independent chapel had existed at Dylife for some time, before a Methodist one was opened in 1841; a Baptist chapel in 1852; and finally, St David's Anglican church arrived in 1856. The following year both a vicarage and school were opened.

Cottages were scattered throughout the area of the mines. In particular, there were rows of cottages and allotments towards the western end of the village at Rhanc-y-myndd, and others at the eastern end known as Bryn Golau. The new mining company built many houses to accommodate its employees, and it also paid £25 a year towards the costs of the school. By 1864, the population was teetering around the 1,000 mark.

There were three hostelries in the village: the Llwyn y Grug Inn, the Star Inn, and the Drop Inn. The innkeeper at the Llwyn y Grug also ran a grocery and a butcher's shop, and there was a post office and a smithy. For entertainment, there was a monthly fair at which traders from Machynlleth, Llanidloes and Llanbrynmair would set up stalls. The fair at Llanbrynmair was particularly known for cobbling. Another form of popular entertainment was cockfighting

Much of Dylife's mining machinery was powered by enormous waterwheels, including Rhod Goch, or the Red Wheel, seen here. With a diameter of 63 feet, it was possibly the largest such wheel in Wales. The man at the centre of the photograph indicates its scale

Photograph courtesy of Powysland Museum

View through the church gate at Dylife. Although the graveyard and graves remain, the church itself was demolished in 1962

Photograph courtesy of Stephen Fisk

and the village had its own cockpit where bets were made and money exchanged.

At Dylife, or any other mining village for that matter, there were many health concerns. However, there was little access to doctors for the ordinary working man, most of whom died tragically young. At Dylife there would undoubtedly have been a high incidence of lead poisoning, not only in the miners but in those working above ground on the dressing floors. Stephen Fisk notes:

> *The inhabitants of Dylife would have absorbed lead through the food they ate, the water they drank, the air they breathed, and the soil and dust they touched. Once inside the human body lead inflicts severe damage on the production of blood, the internal organs, the enzyme systems, the nervous system, and the brain. At high levels lead will cause coma, convulsions and death.*

The mines at Dylife reached their highest level of production in 1862, when 2,571 tonnes of lead ore were sold and profits of about £1,000 a month were made. After this the productivity of the mines steadily declined, as did the price of lead, and in 1873 the Manchester businessmen decided to sell up. During the next decade two other companies attempted to maintain some informal mining until 1886; and from that year to 1901 a local man, Even Evans, continued to coordinate a limited amount of production, employing 20 to 30 men. Evans invested in the building of a tram road, proving that he had both imagination and a vision of a future for the village. However, he lacked the necessary capital to maintain the mines, the tram, and all the other associated paraphernalia. So, in 1901, the mines finally closed. And with nobody else stepping forward to continue production, they soon became flooded and abandoned.

As a new century dawned, yet another village was being lost and its inhabitants were faced with the cruel decision of either remaining to eke out what existence they could from agriculture, or uprooting for a better life elsewhere. Many headed for the United States, following a pattern of emigration that had begun earlier in the nineteenth century. On one day alone, it is recorded that 99 people left Llanbrynmair, bound for America. Other people, especially those with additional skills, sought employment in the coal mines of South Wales or England. A few people carried on living at Dylife after 1901. In 1921, there were 12 pupils on the school register, but in 1925 the school was closed. The last marriage at St David's church took place in 1915, with the last christening in 1926. The church was demolished in 1962. Abandoned cottages fell into ruin and slowly disappeared from the landscape. No doubt their stonework was removed to enhance the walls of local farms. Two of the chapels were converted into private houses, which still exist today. Another surviving building of interest is the Star Inn, which continues to provide refreshments, meals and overnight accommodation.

The Glyndwr Way, a long-distance walk that cuts across the middle of Wales, passes very close to the remnants of Dylife. As well as a mere handful of surviving properties, you can still discern the shadows of several other buildings; disused mine workings; the pits where the great waterwheels once stood; reservoirs, and the leats that carried water down to the village and mines. In places the path follows the route taken by the farmers as they took their horse drawn carts laden with lead ore towards the port of Derwenlas. The walk, however, does not go as far as the port and diverges into the town of Machynlleth, where in 1404 Owain Glyndwr convened a Welsh parliament and proclaimed himself Prince of Wales.

The ghostly remains of one of a series of cottages dotted around the area of Stoke Bottom. This one can be found very near the disused quarry

3

THE POWER
OF WATER

At the beginning of the twentieth century, tiny hamlets and villages existed all over the rural landscape, as the power of water was harnessed to turn the wheels of industry – albeit on a very localised and small scale. Rivers everywhere provided the power for mills and factories, many of which were isolated concerns, the ruins of which can be found on riverbanks the length and breadth of Britain. Others nestled at the heart of tiny communities, so small in fact that even though they might only have disappeared relatively recently in historical terms, there is little available information about them.

One such village was Stoke Bottom in the Mendip Hills of Somerset, near the coal mining town of Radstock. Although this was largely a coal mining area, the local craft at Stoke Bottom was papermaking. Today, you can still see traditional papermaking processes being practiced at the nearby Wookey Hole paper mill. Particulars of the Wookey Hole mill published in 1858 stated that:

> The Mill is placed at the head of the River Axe, which takes its rise in the Mendip Hills, and percolates through the rock into the mill-head, which is a reservoir of considerable extent formed in a natural cavern under the hill. The stream has a fall of 40 feet, and gives power equal to 40 horses by means of a Turbine waterwheel.

Papermaking was a traditional art in this area of Somerset, but the mill at Wookey Hole became so successful that many of its smaller competitors in the surrounding area were forced to close. The skilled papermakers from other settlements would then walk daily to Wookey in order to secure employment. We can only surmise as to whether or not this situation helped to bring about the decline of Stoke Bottom, but evidently while some villages flourished and grew, others slowly disappeared from the landscape.

If you visit the lost village today you will find the ruins of what appears to be the mill itself and several cottages, both in the woods by Stoke Bottom Farm, and by crossing a field to a lane where there are further cottages near a disused quarry. Local people rumour that some of the cottages were still in occupation as late as the 1960s or even 1970s, but nobody seems really certain of the facts. There was also a local Georgian mansion house called Stoke House, set in its own landscaped gardens, which is said to have been abandoned around 1905. The mansion house itself, which was demolished before the Second World War, was reputed to be haunted by a young lady of the house who is said to have thrown herself out of an upstairs bedroom window after suffering from a broken heart. Therefore, Stoke Bottom truly is a 'ghost village' in more than one respect.

On the other side of Somerset in the upland region between Exmoor and the Brendon Hills is another lost village of which similarly very little is known. Today, the ghostly remains of a small village known as Clicket – little more than a hamlet – can be found just outside the Luxborough parish boundary. In a remote and often gloomy valley, you will discover the remains of a mill and several cottages, one of which is larger than the rest and is believed to have been a meeting house. As well as buildings, a search through the undergrowth reveals the site of the waterwheel, two millstones, and a tiny picturesque packhorse bridge, still in very good condition. All around the area natural springs of water in the hillsides create little rivulets known as 'goyals' to Exmoor people. The main stream into which these goyals flow is the Chernet River, which runs through the area where the village once stood and along the valley to Timberscombe. As well as the mill itself, there are the remains of a weir and a millpond. Boundary walls appear to have ancient hedge beech trees growing out of them, one of which is reputed to be among the largest in the county, although Clicket is not actually as ancient as the ruinous scene might suggest.

Clicket is in a deep valley to the south of Timberscombe. There are no actual roads leading to it, so the best approach is to drive up from Dunster towards Luxborough. This will take you through

Part of the lost Somerset and Dorset Canal, very near the ghost village of Stoke Bottom in the Mendip Hills of Somerset. This ambitious scheme would have linked Bath to Christchurch, but only 13 miles were ever completed. The section in the photograph would have gone from Nettlebridge to Frome along the Mells valley, and a look on a map illustrates how invaluable that would have been to the paper mill at Stoke Bottom

At Wookey Hole paper was hung over hair ropes or laid flat on hessian in the drying lofts. The ventilation shutters needed skilled regulation

Photograph reproduced from Wookey Hole guide book with the permission of Daniel Medley, general manager, Wookey Hole Caves

a large wooded area of plantations, known as Croydon Hill, the summit of which is Bat's Castle standing at 365 metres – not to be confused with Bat's Castle Settlement to the east, which presents a lost village from an earlier age. Along the road, as you begin your descent, there is an Exmoor National Park fingerpost pointing the way to Clicket through a field gate on the right. You can also drive on towards Nurcott Farm and find a suitable car park, and there is also some parking on the path above Thorne Farm.

There are several footpaths but an Ordnance Survey map is essential, from which you will see a network of well-worn, centuries old tracks that would have been used by drovers, lime burners, quarrymen, school children and farmers bringing their corn to and from Clicket Mill. Alternatively, the remains actually lie within the grounds of Allercott Farm, where you can rent holiday cottages and explore the valley at leisure. So although there is a series of public footpaths, be aware that some of the village is on private property.

It might seem improbable now but 100 years ago Clicket was a busy little community, which had probably been in existence for around 400 years. In 1851, the census recorded a miller and five other families; about 40 people in total. Most of the men were farm labourers, although one is recorded as being a quarryman who worked at Allercott quarry, while another was marked down as being a lumberman. It is easy to see how timber provided a source of employment in the village, as the valley is bordered by substantial plantations. Also, the Ordnance Survey map reveals disused quarries liberally strewn over quite a wide surrounding area, while of course farming was the lifeblood of many lush Exmoor valleys. There are also lime kilns in the local landscape. So, from the census, we can deduce that the community existed and thrived for a number of reasons other than simply because of the existence of the mill.

Over the years, Clicket Mill has been referred to by several names, including Hydron and Beckham, and at the time of the 1851 census, the miller was a certain William Langdon. It was certainly in existence during Elizabethan times. As well as the mill building itself, the remains of the miller's house can still be seen and it was here that Langdon lived with his wife and five children. Apparently, the household also supported his simple sister-in-law and a 14-year-old servant boy, called James Gadd.

Clicket Mill was a corn mill to which local farmers would have sent their corn to be ground by the miller. They would have sent their produce by pack animal along the various pack horse trails. These animals would normally have been donkeys or horses; or possibly oxen may have sometimes been employed. Because of the steep valley terrain, it is very unlikely that heavy farm carts were ever used in such operations. Langdon himself had two donkeys of his own called Dick and Short, which provided a collection service to some farmers. They would negotiate the valley tracks to nearby farms and pick up any corn that required milling. It was said that they knew the route so well that they were able to do this unattended, although it is more likely that the young James Gadd would have kept a watchful eye on the situation. After milling, the resultant flour, or 'middlings' as some of it was known, would have been loaded into panniers and returned along the same paths.

But there is no doubt that as with papermaking at Stoke Bottom, small corn mills would slowly have gone out of business as they were unable to compete with larger concerns that offered better facilities and mechanisation. Clicket's difficult terrain and uneasy access would have made it less appealing to farmers in the modern age as well. So, around 1900, the mill finally fell silent and was abandoned, quickly falling into disrepair. From then until the First World War, it became the playground of local children, but its last residents were an elderly couple who had been evicted from their cottage. Sadly, with nowhere else to go, they took refuge in the old mill and lived there for about a year in a building with no windows or doors. To them, this was preferable than being forced to live at the poorhouse at Williton, which was considered to be a humiliation for the independent people of Exmoor. But eventually the old man died and it is believed that his wife finally succumbed to the poorhouse, where she lived out the rest of her days.

Of the other buildings in the village it is recorded that the remains of the larger house at Clicket was a meeting house. Whether or not it was also a family home at the same time is unsure, although it almost certainly would have been. There was no church or chapel in the village, the nearest being at either Timberscombe or Luxborough Churchtown. So religious gatherings would have been held periodically at the meeting house, evidence of at least one of which is known from a magazine of the Bible Christians from 1851. It was recorded by Pastor S. Crocker that around 70 people attended the meeting. As the village supported only 40, it is assumed that

A millstone amongst the foliage of Clicket, where once stood a thriving corn mill

Photograph courtesy of Dennis Corner

A group of ramblers stop and look at the ruins of Clicket, and enjoy the solitude of a location that was once a bustling hive of activity

Photograph courtesy of Dennis Corner

the remainder of this congregation would almost certainly have been drawn from the local farming community. Edward Cording, who presided over the meeting, was a farmer himself who farmed along the valley towards Timberscombe Common at Croydon. It is therefore probable that some of the farm labourers dwelling at Clicket would have been in his employ.

At this meeting, the gathered throng enjoyed addresses delivered by Pastor Crocker and brethren Conibeer and Hicks. It was described as a "tea meeting on behalf of the Missionary Society," and Pastor Crocker wrote that it had been a "blessed meeting, and the friends exerted themselves nobly." A collection for the Missionary Society amounted to one pound, thirteen shillings and three pence.

Bible Christians, or Bryanite preachers, had first entered this part of west Somerset in the early 1820s, led by a lady called Mary Mason, known as the Maiden Preacher. They established cottage fellowships for prayer and preaching, and this was undoubtedly what was taking place at Clicket. One of the most important fellowships in the area was started in the shopkeeper's cottage at Timberscombe. Edward Cording and his elder brother, James, arrived on the scene in 1833. Their father John had been a prosperous farmer at Bathealton who had moved to Upton in 1817. John had become involved with the new Bryanite preachers and his two sons were inspired by his enthusiasm and became preachers themselves. After the death of John, the two brothers obtained the lease of the manor and farm called Croydon Hall. This house sat along the side of the valley below Timberscombe on the way to Clicket, so for the next 60 years passing preachers were always welcome and Clicket would have been a regular place for cottage meetings.

Edward was very much responsible for building a chapel in Timberscombe, which was opened in 1836. James died at the end of 1836 but Edward lived until 1886. He was a local preacher for 52 years and circuit steward from 1840 to 1869. He gave up farming at Croydon in 1876 and went to live at Timberscombe in a house he had built himself, just opposite the chapel. However, by 1900, attendance at the chapel had dropped away, and the reasons for this mirror the situation at Clicket: basically, economic depression and depopulation was beginning to take their toll. Local mines and slate quarries were closing and the reports from the circuit pastors spoke of young people, often entire families, moving away to seek a better life elsewhere. In 1907, the Bible Christian Church became part of the United Methodist Church, and in 1932 this amalgamated with the Wesleyans and the Primitives to become the present day Methodist Church, and a chapel is still going strong in Timberscombe today.

Other social activities at Clicket are known to have included a juvenile band and an annual club walk on Whit Monday, complete with floral staves. But as well as having no church or chapel, the village had no shops, the nearest being at Luxborough. Nor did Clicket have a school, so the children had to walk each day along the valley track to Timberscombe, following the route of the stream. This journey took them through South Cleeve Grove, Black Well Wood, and past Bougam Farm. It was a distance of nearly two miles through difficult terrain, against the uncertainty of Exmoor's notorious weather. A sunny aspect during the walk to school in the morning could have turned into a torrential downpour by the time of the return journey in the afternoon. And as the fog on Exmoor is legendary, the necessity to stick together and be aware of their surroundings would have been drummed into the children at a very young age.

In the 1851 census, there were nine children described as 'scholars', although some of these were infrequent attendees. In an article for the *West Somerset Free Press,* local historian Hilary Binding quoted an entry in the Timberscombe school logbook from October 1879 which said that a certain John Webber from Clicket (spelt Clicott) had called at the schoolhouse on account of a summons he had received. At this meeting he was informed of the poor school attendance of his two sons, Edwin and Jesse. Edwin had only attended 14 times during the Harvest Quarter and in another period, out of a possible 140 days, he had only attended on 41 occasions. And as if that was not bad enough, Mr Webber was then told that during the same period Jesse had only attended on 33 occasions.

Hilary Binding also wrote of a photograph in her possession, which illustrates some of the last people to live in Clicket. "The men are clearly working men but they have a rakish air," she wrote. "One sports a chequered tie, watch chain and straw boater above the apron which points to him being the miller. I have been told that another of the men in the photograph had to leave the country fairly quickly following a brawl in which a man was killed."

In the Somerset County archives, the last census of the nineteenth century mentions Kiln Close and Quarry Close, which supports the idea that Clicket was more of a village than the scattered remnants we see today might suggest. It also records the names of people who lived there, names that are still commonplace in the area, among them: James Hole, the Reverend Henry John Taylor, John Cole, Martin Williams, James Williams, Robert Tarr, and Ursula Tarr. The latter causes us to immediately think of one of Exmoor's best loved landmarks, the Tarr Steps which ford the River Barle near Liscombe. As for when the last people left the village, little is known, although several sources tell of a lady from Clicket who, during the 1950s, walked to work each day from the village to Porlock on the Somerset coast, a journey of at least seven miles, depending on her route. This would have been a gruelling and hilly journey, the most likely route of which would have taken her through Timberscombe, Wooton Courtenay, Huntscott, Luccombe and Horner. The return journey at the end of the long working day would have been even worse, as it was an upward climb for much of the way.

The record of one Clicket lady was printed as an obituary in a local paper. The date of the piece and the journal are unsure, although it was probably printed around 1977 in the *West Somerset Free Press*. However, this obituary recorded the death of Mrs Lily E. Bryant, and states:

> *News of the death in Bristol on November 9th, of Mrs Lily Elizabeth Bryant, recalls a long family association with the Washford district, and Mrs Bryant's own contribution as a caterer at many social events. The older generation, especially those connected with the Methodist Church, will remember one of her specialties – rabbit pie suppers.*

The obituary explains that:

> *Mrs Bryant, born in 1889 in the now vanished little village of Clicket, near Timberscombe, was the last surviving child of George and Rachel Burge. In 1914 she married Mr William John Bryant, eldest son of John and Emma Bryant, of Bilbrook. Mr W. J. Bryant was for many years a local preacher in the former Williton Methodist circuit. While living in the Washford district, Mrs Bryant was a keen worker for the Methodist Church, the WI, Mother's Union and Royal British Legion. She worked for many years as the confectionery cook at the Bungalow Café, Minehead, and also as cook at Woolworths in Minehead.*

Eventually, Mr and Mrs Bryant left the district for Fishponds in Bristol, to reside with their youngest daughter, Barbara. Mr Bryant died there in 1971 and the following year Mrs Bryant moved to Abbotswood, Yate, to live with her eldest daughter, Lilian. In December 1976, due to poor health, and on medical advice, she entered Newton House, Cadbury Heath, where she died after a very short illness. Was therefore, Lily Elizabeth Bryant (nee Burge), the last surviving resident of the lost village of Clicket?

The valley in which Clicket once stood, although beautiful, can be dark and damp, so it is easy to understand why its people chose to abandon it. The lady who walked to Porlock each day illustrates the fact that the residents of Clicket would have been aware of the outside world, and the Bible Christians recorded how local people were moving away in search of a better life. To young men and women, this gloomy valley must have seemed like the back of beyond. There was little here to tempt them to stay, particularly when a better life with better prospects could be offered virtually anywhere else.

From the start of the twentieth century many small rural villages became depopulated as their prevalent industries went into steady decline; and some, like Stoke Bottom or Clicket, disappeared from the maps completely. The sound of pack animals as they trudged along ancient tracks towards Clicket Mill are today replaced by the wild sounds of Exmoor, such as the roaring of the famous red deer. It is quite appropriate that the site has been returned to nature, considering that the word 'clicket' refers to the copulation of foxes.

Whether or not there will be future Clicket's is very unlikely. Today, we have an affluent element to our society that purchases rural cottages as second homes and weekend retreats. Sadly, if rural people today find it hard to live in their ancestral communities because there is no work available, this does not spell the end of the village, as there will be a ready army of city professionals armed with hefty bonuses, ready to snap up their homes. Exmoor and the Brendon Hills are perfect examples of this scenario, as one or two villages are now almost completely owned by people from outside. But in a sense, are these not lost villages in their own right? It is true that the houses remain standing, but rural villages were made of more than just bricks and mortar: villages were often measured by the people who lived in them, their traditions, history, faith, and sense of community.

4

A SORELY-DISTRESSED
COMMUNITY

Some parts of Britain were so remote that even during the Victorian age and early twentieth century they seemed to change very little. They were so remote, in fact, that the people living there would have been largely oblivious to the social changes and improvements taking place in other parts of the realm. The villages covered so far in this book met their demise through the collapse of their mining, industrial, or agricultural base. However, there were more complex reasons as well, such as those factors influencing the abandonment of Mingulay.

Mingulay island, which roughly measures two-and-a-half miles by one-and-a-half miles, covers an area of 1,581 acres (640 hectares). It is the second most southerly of the group of islands known as the Bishop's Isles, which lie off the southern tip of the Outer Hebrides, south of Barra, and which include Vatersay, Sandray, Lingay, Pabbay, and Berneray – the last of which is the only significant landmass south of our subject. Make a note of these names, as several feature in the following narrative.

Many small Scottish islands were deserted during the nineteenth century, as well as villages on the larger islands of the Western Isles, Orkney Islands and Shetland Isles. Some of these settlements could be regarded as villages, while others comprised of a few scattered crofts. In our definition, if a community had such things as a school and a church, as Mingulay did, it can be regarded as a village. So just as Morwellham Quay represented a number of other lost villages in the Tamar Valley, and Dylife the abandoned mining communities of mid-Wales, Mingulay is representative of numerous island settlements that were disappearing around 1900. What might appear strange is that people should wish to live in

On Mingulay peat was plentiful and used for fuel. This photograph shows peat diggers on an unspecified Hebridean island

Photograph by Cherry Kearton, reproduced from the book With Nature and a Camera by Richard Kearton, published in 1898 by Cassell and Company

such a remote location in the first place. The island is surrounded by high cliffs, with only one possible landing place on the east coast where a bay is enclosed by an amphitheatre of hills. The village was situated at the head of this bay, but for much of the year the treacherous sea conditions effectively cut the islanders off from the rest of civilisation.

Surprisingly, the island was an extremely good place to live. It had supported human settlement since the Neolithic times. Its people were very close-knit and self-sufficient, and while things were going well their isolation from the rest of Britain was no particular handicap. There was an abundance of peat, which could be used for fuel. The grass on the hills was suitable for grazing cattle and sheep. The sea provided fish and the cliffs teemed with colonies of seabirds bursting with eggs. These colonies also attracted a trickle of Victorian tourists interested in ornithology, although not to the same extent as the more accessible islands of the Outer Hebrides.

So what went wrong? The truth is that Mingulay continued to prosper while its population remained constant. Before 1841, the only known population figure was 52, recorded in 1764. The island could clearly support this number of people. Most of the Bishop's Isles were owned by a clan chief called General MacNeil of Barra who, during the 1830s, was facing financial ruin and the prospect of bankruptcy. He began a process of evicting people from one or two of these islands. Some of the people were forced to live on Barra itself in order to work at the General's kelp works at Northbay. The islands from which they came were then given over for the grazing of sheep: much more profitable to the MacNeils than any revenue provided from crofting. The enterprise failed and from around 1837 these islands were steadily repopulated – all that is but one: the island of Sandray.

Sandray had a similar population to Mingulay, and the MacNeils continued to reserve it for sheep. Some of its population emigrated to Mingulay, which had already seen a partial growth after the eviction of its other neighbours. By 1841, Mingulay's population had swelled to 114 and continued to grow, peaking in the 1880s at around 160. In little over 100 years, the island's population had trebled and its limited resources were coming under increasing pressure.

Ben Buxton, an authority on Mingulay, has written extensively on the subject, including the book *Mingulay: An island and its people* and a chapter about the island in the book, *The Decline and Fall of St Kilda*. He writes that:

The rising population also led to overcrowding in the village, which became insanitary, and there were outbreaks of diseases such as typhoid, measles and influenza. It was often impossible to get to Barra to summon the doctor, or, just as importantly, the priest. The rising population, lack of land and problems of access led to a few families moving to crofts at Garrygall in Barra in 1883.

Pressure on the land caused by this population rise meant that the inhabitants had to find other means of supplementing their incomes. Fishing was the obvious choice and the period coincided with the growth of a fishing port at Castlebay on the larger island of Barra. Up until this point, fishing had largely aided the island's self-sufficiency. Their catch – usually by line – would have been white fish, such as cod or ling, which would be cured on the rocks. Some of their catch was sold to the fishing industries of Glasgow and Northern Ireland.

As a port, Castlebay developed because of the plentiful herring that shoaled in Scottish waters, while for the people of Mingulay it provided opportunities for selling fish. There was, however, a problem: the island had only one place from which boats could be launched or landed, and that was on the beach at Mingulay Bay. Rocks at either side of the bay, which in the past had been used to land people and goods, certainly could not accommodate fishing boats. The broad sweep of the bay opened it up to the elements, providing little shelter from the wind or swell. Boats at anchor here could easily be driven on to the rocks. Any boats that did attempt to use the beach could only be launched by wading into the choppy, freezing waves to at least chest height, an operation made impossible for much of the year because of the atrocious sea conditions.

Ben Buxton notes how one visitor to the island reported the problem of landing supplies: "It is no unusual occurrence for them to have to throw their bags of meal into the sea and drag them ashore by means of a rope." The visitor further suggested that, "it is easier to reach America than to get there."

All of this put Mingulay fishermen at a disadvantage, as they were unable to begin fishing before March or April, whereas their rivals from Barra could cast off in February. Also, herring had to be caught using nets as opposed to line, and this required larger boats. To compete in the herring industry several men from Mingulay operated suitable craft, but as they were too large to use the beach they were anchored at Castlebay. Several other fishermen based themselves on the nearby island of Berneray during the fishing season, as access was easier. However, this meant being away from home for lengthy periods of time. Of those without their own fishing vessels, some were able to secure seasonal employment aboard herring boats from Barra, and women from all over the islands sought work as herring gutters. This also involved working away from home during the summer months at places on the east coast of Scotland, such as Peterhead, following the fish as they migrated.

This growing dependency on fishing, coupled with the rise in the island's population, meant there was less time being spent on traditional island activities, such as crofting and fowling – the very activities that had made the community self-reliant. If they were to compete at all, the problem of finding a suitable place to anchor their boats was paramount: not only to support the fishing boats but in order to land the increasing amount of supplies the villagers needed now they were becoming less self-sufficient. One answer to this problem would have been the building of a boat slip, but the islanders had neither the knowledge nor finances to accomplish this.

In 1890, a government commission was informed of the problem of access to the village and, in 1896, its inhabitants sent a petition to the Secretary of State for Scotland, signed by all of the male population, appealing for help in constructing a "boat-slip with a boat-hauling convenience." The petition concluded with the hope that "your lordship will lend a favourable ear to the cry of a sorely-distressed community."

Ben Buxton goes on to explain that in the following year, the Congested Districts Board was established by the Scottish Office to promote economic development in crofting areas:

The Board took on the problem and, having ruled out a pier or boat slip because of the exposed nature of the bay and its sandy floor, proposed a crane or derrick for hoisting boats right out of the water. However, this scheme was downgraded, presumably because of cost, and in 1901 a derrick for loading and unloading people, animals and goods into and out of boats was installed near the landing place. While this may have been useful, the main problem, that of the boats remained.

While all of this was going on, village life was maintained. A school was opened in 1859 by the Ladies' Highland Association. Presumably, education before this date was provided in the home, as were religious services. Without a doubt, the access to formal education and the practice of working away at mainland ports would have given the villager's some idea of the outside world – and the standard of life enjoyed beyond their island retreat. In 1898, a substantial Roman Catholic chapel was built to administer to the island's predominant faith. The building of the chapel came courtesy of the See of Argyll and the Isles, a project founded in 1878 and funded by a wealthy merchant from Castlebay. This was the first chapel on the island for centuries. It provided both an area in which to hold services and rooms for the visiting priest who, during the summer months, would come monthly from Barra and less frequently at other times of the year.

In the 1890s, the landowner was Lady Gordon Cathcart. Like the MacNeils before her, she did not feel there was any profit to be made from crofting. Fishing was a much more viable proposition; and besides, she had just paid for the improvement to the pier at Castlebay. Lady Cathcart would only permit the crofters at Castlebay to cultivate small plots of land: just enough to grow a few potatoes, but not enough to make them independent. This lack of land effectively forced them into the fishing industry. So with no new crofts being provided for the growing population, and no house building undertaken, the people were living in increasingly squalid, overcrowded conditions.

A few nautical miles to the north of Mingulay, but south of Barra, lay the slightly larger island of Vatersay, which had traditionally been crofted before the evictions earlier in the century. Many descendants of those who had lived on Vatersay now lived on Barra, probably even a few on Mingulay itself. Aware of the abundance of space on this sister island, the cottars of Castlebay sent an appeal for land as early as 1883, which was rejected. The island was being managed as one large farm and the only people living there were the farmer, his family and workforce.

In 1894, there was an interesting development, as a government commission designated certain areas to be suitable for crofting, among them Vatersay. However, Lady Cathcart refused to comply, maintaining that crofting tenants were poor rent payers. Her Ladyship wanted all available men to work in the fishing industry. Fuelled no doubt by the government's decision on crofting and Lady

Mingulay Bay, photographed in June 2006. The island is surrounded by high cliffs, so this was the only possible landing place. The village was situated at the head of this bay and for much of the year the treacherous sea conditions effectively cut the islanders off from the rest of civilisation

Photograph courtesy of Tony Kinghorn

Cathcart's total disregard for them, their families and heritage, a group of men who became known as 'raiders' began to turn the tide of history.

The first raids took place on farms at Northbay and Eoligarry on Barra, where men began to mark out crofts. Subsequently, this land was purchased by the Congested Districts Board for the purpose of crofting. The first raid on Vatersay was in 1900 when a group of Castlebay cottars invaded the island and similarly began to mark out areas for crofting. In 1902, the Board bought up this land and made it available to the cottars for growing potatoes. Until now, they had not really encroached on the farm itself, but in 1905 when the lease on the farm came up for renewal – and their appeal for land was again turned down – the cottars began to mark out crofts near the farm itself. Ben Buxton writes:

The Mingulay people no doubt followed these events with interest. By 1905 the community was in decline: the photographs taken by Robert Adam show that some buildings had been abandoned, and Morag Campbell Finlayson wrote 'we spend the winter months lonely and dull... we shall be like prisoners during the bad weather... I am hoping to leave Mingulay soon'. (She did so shortly afterwards.) In July 1906 four Mingulay cottars joined a large number from Castlebay in a raid on Vatersay, and, for the first time, some of the desperate Barra men began to build huts in the vicinity of the farm buildings. In August Michael Campbell attempted to build a hut at Ledaig, Castlebay, but desisted when the local crofters asked him to, and later in the year he built the hut near the farm on Vatersay. In January 1907 he and others from Mingulay moved into the hut, and they were followed by a stream of other Mingulay settlers throughout 1907.

The island of Sandray, from where a number of Mingulay's population had originated, was still being used for grazing sheep, and was inhabited by a solitary shepherd. So a number of men raided the island and set about constructing stone and thatch houses at Sheader. Here, a sheltered bay enabled them to fish for lobsters. They sent an appeal to the Congested Districts Board asking for crofting land, as it was becoming impossible to exist on their own island: even fishing was regarded as more dangerous there than at other locations.

Attempting to solve various such problems around the Bishop's Isles, the Board offered to buy the land on Vatersay from Lady Cathcart, but the price she demanded was too high and instead she took legal action against 11 of the raiders, including five men from Mingulay. In June 1908, this action resulted in 10 of the raiders being summoned to Edinburgh to appear before the Court of Sessions. They were subsequently sentenced to two months imprisonment. However, the case was surrounded by media interest, which both highlighted and sympathized with the plight of the island crofters. Much of this interest was achieved by a man from Mingulay, Neil MacPhee. Although not one of the men under summons himself, he acted as their spokesman, writing intelligent and thought-provoking correspondences to the press. These did an enormous amount to sway public opinion in their favour.

All of this, however, placed the Congested Districts Board in an awkward position. It seemed increasingly the case that once a raid had taken place, they would simply buy up the land in question for the crofters. Obviously this could not continue for two reasons: the first being that it encouraged disgruntled crofters to strike when and where they liked; and secondly, because the landowners were becoming more unrealistic about the price of their land. Nevertheless, due to public sympathy, Lady Cathcart appears to have had a change of heart over Vatersay: an agreement was reached and the crofters were given an early release from prison.

Having secured Vatersay in 1909, the Board created 58 new crofts in four townships. Over the next few years all of the islands south of Vatersay were systematically abandoned. Berneray was vacated in 1910, followed by Pabbay and Sandray in 1911. Not everyone from Mingulay wished to leave their ancestral island home, but it was an inevitability, especially after the school was closed and the teacher transferred to a new school on Vatersay in 1910. The last reluctant few finally left Mingulay in the summer of 1912.

Today, the island remains uninhabited and the school, the chapel and other village buildings lie in ruin. Those who visit the islands south of Vatersay now go to see the colonies of puffins, gannets and other seabirds that thrive in this remote corner of Britain. Others might go out of curiosity, and to wonder why a land which happily sustained human life for thousands of years was so completely and irreversibly deserted in such a short period of time.

Remains of the old school house on Mingulay which was finally closed in 1910 when the teacher was transferred to a new school on Vatersay

Photograph courtesy of Paul Store

These cottages on Vatersay were no doubt abandoned at the time of the evictions during the nineteenth century

Photograph courtesy of Calum McRoberts

Hallsands today: the shingle beach has totally gone and the few remaining ruins sit precariously on the edge of the rocks. Perhaps future storms will one day claim what remains of these?

Photograph courtesy of Humphrey Bolton

5

THE CRUEL SEA

As an island nation, villages and even towns along Britain's battered coastline have been under threat from coastal erosion for centuries. However, coastal erosion caused by the ravages of the ocean is not the only factor that has played a part in the abandonment of coastal communities. In terms of general history, perhaps the most famous coastal disappearances were at Kenfig in south Wales, devoured by sand dunes cast up from the Severn estuary, and at Dunwich, a major sea port in Suffolk, slowly demolished by the shrinking shoreline. But from the twentieth century, Hallsands on the south coast of Devon remains the most studied and perhaps controversial of coastal devastations.

On the night of 26 January 1917, the village of Hallsands was destroyed during a severe storm. The village had been protected by a large pebble ridge and on that fateful night exceptionally high waves came pounding over it, crashing into the houses. The village had become vulnerable because sand and gravel had been dredged from the seabed in order to enlarge the naval dockyards at Devonport, consequently reducing the shingle beach.

The few houses and hotel that make up the modern hamlet of Hallsands can be found near Start Point, which itself is close to Prawle Point, the southernmost extremity of Devon. Visitors today can no longer visit the old village, but it can be studied from a viewing platform. Looking down from this vantage point you immediately ask the question: "why was a village built in such a precarious spot in the first place?" But the fact is Hallsands was not always as close to the water's edge as it is today.

The houses were built on a shelf of rock that protruded from the base of the cliffs. These rocks provided a relatively flat surface, but presumably any uneven areas were levelled off with compacted sand. This ledge hovered significantly above the water line and was never less than 10 feet from the sea – even at its highest level. In the main, the village formed one narrow street along this ledge, with houses on either side of the street, while a sea wall provided extra protection from the English Channel. Some of the houses even used the cliff face as their back wall, which although not uncommon on the south coast, seems rather reckless. Every boy scout knows that you should never pitch your shelter beneath a cliff, for obvious reasons. Apart from the possibility of landslides and falling rocks, for which this shoreline is renowned, its location beneath east-facing cliffs suggest that on days when the South Hams basked in sunshine, Hallsands itself would have been enveloped in shadowy gloom for much of the day. But on the positive side, the overhanging cliffs offered the village protection against westerly gales.

The only reason why a village would be built in such an unlikely location is because the livelihood of its occupants depended on it – and Hallsands depended on fishing. Along the rocky coastline between Hallsands and Salcombe, there are few places from which fishermen could operate, let alone live. Then there was the little matter of Skerries Bank, a veritable garden of Eden for fishing folk, still today fished for sole, mackerel, gurnard, bass and other varieties of fish, which absolutely abounded here in offshore depressions known as 'pits'. Hallsands was about as close to these pits as you could get.

As the village did not have a harbour, and was therefore unsuitable for trawlers, the villagers relied heavily on inshore crab and lobster fishing, or 'potting' as it was known. But in order to catch crabs and lobsters, they first had to gather bait. For this they did not have to go far, as the fish used for baiting the pots could be hauled in from the beach. Basically, rowing boats would take massive nets called 'seine nets' out to sea, following instructions from a man who sat on the clifftop called a 'hillman', who would be on the look out for suitable shoals. A purpose-built rowing boat was used which had a platform at the stern on which the net was carefully packed. The boat would leave the shore with the net paying out behind it and would follow a short semi-circular course around the shoal back to the shore. Then it was pulled at each end. Every man and woman would receive a share of the spoils. Each man would receive one share of the catch and each woman two-thirds of a share. The owner of the boat and nets would receive three shares. Seine fishing was very much a communal activity that brought the entire village together, and for many young lads it was their first experience of fishing.

The catches would be mostly mullet and bass during spring and early summer, and mackerel in late summer. Only certain fish would be suitable for crab bait, so the remainder would either be eaten by the local families, sold to hawkers who would take them around the nearby farms and hamlets, or would be sent to London by train from Kingsbridge seven miles away where it would largely end up in Billingsgate market. Only bass, mullet and salmon were sent up-country: mackerel deteriorates quickly and would have been immediately sold locally. Because Hallsands did not have a harbour, the beach was effectively the village work place. Here, crab and lobster pots would be stacked, nets dried, and boats would sit upon the shingle waiting to be launched.

Several other methods of fishing were practised from Hallsands, as well as seine fishing and potting. These included tuck netting, trammel netting and longlining. Tuck netting, or drag netting as it was known elsewhere, was similar to seine fishing, except instead of catching shoals of fish that were observed moving close to the shoreline, the nets would be taken much further out to sea. And instead of encircling the shoal, the tuck net would form a wall beneath the water, which was then slowly dragged back to shore. During this process, teams of men would work on the beach, and in a special hauling boat.

The trammel was a static net that was kept in an upright position below the water line. Lead weights would anchor its bottom to the seabed, while cork floats would keep its top near the surface. The net formed two layers, which entrapped any fish that swam into it headlong. Longlining, on the other hand, was employed to catch fish that actually lived along the seabed, such as ray at the Skerries and conger eel near the cliffs. The line was a baited piece of rope, and after being anchored to the bottom for the required period of time, it would be hoisted up to the boat, where the waiting crew would pull the fish aboard. Apparently conger eel, which were particularly good as crab bait, would be subdued with a mallet before being hauled into the boat to stop them thrashing about and causing injury or damage.

Much of the catch from all of these different fishing methods was used to bait the pots that were set offshore to ensnare crabs

Hallsands photographed in 1885. Above: the beach was narrow at this time, due to natural causes, and Wilson's Rock appears to sit half in and half out of the water. Below: a lady with several children in front of her house, gives a good idea of how the beach was used as the work place of the fishermen. Hardly an inch seems unused

Photographs courtesy of Plymouth Records & Archives

and lobsters. Once caught, the crabs were either kept alive in large storage pots from where they were periodically picked up by a crab smack from Southampton, or they were taken to Kingsbridge railway station to be sent to London. Catching crabs was one thing; however, selling them was quite a different matter. This aspect of their business was in the hands of agents in London. The crabs, lobsters and other fish sent from Hallsands had to compete with those sent from many other fishing communities, so they often found themselves at the mercy of unscrupulous traders.

The crab pots were made from willows, many of which were brought from the Somerset Levels. But as a coincidence, a nearby spring running through the above valley created perfect conditions for growing them. Each family was able to harvest much of their own annual requirement, and men and women alike would weave the finished pots. The spring also provided the village with its water supply. Initially, water would have been collected in buckets after a long trudge up the hill, but around the start of the twentieth century the water was being channelled to the village through bore pipes.

Nobody quite knows how old the village is or when the first people lived here. Early records mention a chapel at Start Point, today noted for its lighthouse. If there was a chapel here around 1500 there is certainly no archeological evidence to indicate where. Hallsands itself is within the parish of Stokenham, and the Stokenham Manor Court Rolls of the early seventeenth century mention it on several occasions, but with different spellings, such as Halesande, Halsands, and Halesands. These unquestionably refer to the same place, and the variety of spellings reflect the fact that few people could read or write at the time, all of which serves to hamper modern investigations and makes some of our assumptions the product of conjecture.

By 1900, there were approximately 160 people in the village living in 37 houses, most of which were owner-occupied. This was unusual to say the least, and how fishing families could afford mortgages is not clear. However, tenants were offered the chance to purchase their properties when the landlord, Sir Robert Newman, died in 1857, and most seized the opportunity.

Hallsands enjoyed similar facilities to most small rural villages of the time. There was a pub named the London Inn, positioned along the main street, which brewed its own ale. Naturally, its clientele largely comprised of local fishermen. The men who ferried the fish to Kingsbridge and other tradesmen visiting the village were able to use the stabling facilities for their horses, while they themselves enjoyed the hospitality within. There was also a shop, with a post office; a bakery; and for spiritual guidance, the mission room.

Several properties were built on top of the cliffs, where there was a coastguard station with a row of cottages to house the men, and just to the north, a Bible Christian chapel that had superceded the mission room as the venue for religious services. The mission room itself became a sort of village hall where people gathered to tell stories, sing sea shanties, dance, and entertain their neighbours from villages like Beesands and Torcross. Here, many people would meet their future marital partners.

One thing the village did not have was a school, the nearest being at Huckham – itself no more than a cluster of farms and cottages a couple of miles inland along twisting lanes. There was no transport, so all the children of the village would congregate in the morning and walk together. In the spring the children would gather primroses and bluebells on the way home for their mothers to brighten up their kitchens. Today, the South Hams are still a delight in spring and summer, with ancient hedgerows and variety of wild flowers.

So village life at Hallsands had many similarities to other rural communities of the day. And what the villagers could not provide for themselves or purchase at the small village shop run by Katie and Louisa Mingo, local traders would bring. The packman, for instance, would visit on his horse, bringing materials, coloured ribbons and cottons. Boots, shoes, underwear and other clothing would be brought on approval by a courier from Tanners of Kingsbridge. Most fishermen had allotments on the cliff top to grow their vegetables, and there was a coal depot along the road to Beesands. Coke to fuel the range was brought from the Kingsbridge Gas Works and there was a steady supply of driftwood along the beach. From an early age, children would drag driftwood up over the shingle for their fathers to cut up with saw or axe. Much of this wood came from shipwrecks and good pieces could be used for carpentry purposes, making shelves or earth closets. Most men in the village never had a bank account. Payment for their catch was either by cash, money order or cheque. Money orders could be cashed in at the post office and local traders were happy to cash the cheques.

Several books have been written about Hallsands and one in particular, *Sisters Against the Sea* by Ruth and Frank Milton, tells the fascinating story of the Trout family. What makes their story particularly compelling is that they included four sisters: Patience, Ella, Clara and Edith. The two oldest sisters, Patience and Ella, supported their father William, mother Eliza Anne, and two younger sisters, by fishing alongside the menfolk of the village after their father was diagnosed with a serious illness which eventually ushered an end to his own working life. The book's co-author, Frank Milton, is the son of Clara Trout, and as such paints a vivid picture of fishing folk during the early twentieth century.

William and Eliza, both from Hallsands, were married in 1892 at Stokenham parish church. He could only afford to take one day off work, so the following day he was back potting again. They acquired their cottage, which was the last dwelling on the seaward side of the main street at the southern end of the village, following the death of a relative, and one of the first improvements William made was to pebbledash the walls, making them damp-proof. With the inexhaustible supply of shingle on the beach, this was a common practice throughout the village. The cottage had two rooms upstairs and two downstairs. The front door opened from a concrete yard into the main room, which was the kitchen. The internal walls were coated with limewash and there were flagstones on the floor covered with coconut matting. At the back of the kitchen was the scullery and, of course, all the houses had outside toilets with buckets.

Throughout the nineteenth century, a number of severe storms affected the south coast of England, one of the worst being recorded in 1891. Hallsands stood up to these well and suffered little more than superficial damage, such as the loosening of roof tiles. So what had changed by 1917 to cause such catastrophic destruction?

Looking at old photographs of the village the reasons become very apparent. Back then, the houses sat neatly at the top of a wide pebble beach; yet today, the remaining ruins cling precariously to the rocks at the cliff's edge as waves lap around them. So what exactly happened to the beach that once provided both protection and a work place for the villagers? Where did it go?

The answer to this question can be found at the naval docks in Devonport 25 miles away. At this time, the Royal Navy was expanding and her iron warships were becoming too large to use the existing facilities. A large civil engineering company owned by

Sir John Jackson was employed by the Admiralty to enlarge these docks. This work would involve laying down huge amounts of concrete for which sand and shingle was required, an abundance of which sat conveniently off the south coast of Devon.

Sir John first set his sights on the estuary of the River Exe, but his ambitions were thwarted by a man called Mark Rolle, who owned much of Exmouth, and was also a major contributor to Conservative Party funds. Whether or not this had any bearing on Jackson's decision to move his operation down the coast is unclear, but in 1910, Jackson himself became the Tory MP for Devonport.

The shingle itself belonged to the Crown and could only be dredged with the permission of the Board of Trade. Prior to presenting his application to the Board, Jackson approached the landowner of a stretch of coast between Tinsey Head and the Bible Christian chapel, just to the north of the village. Armed with the landowner's consent, Jackson made his application, indicating that the quantity of shingle to be extracted would not interfere with the cliffs or adjoining land. The application was accepted with no proviso placed on the amount of shingle that could be removed, although the Board of Trade did include a clause which would enable them to cancel the agreement if, in their opinion, the foreshore defences of the adjacent land was in any way damaged. By charging Jackson's company for the extraction, the government was set to make a good deal of money. It is very unlikely that at any stage in these negotiations the community at Hallsands was ever consulted or even informed of the plans.

In April 1897, the first steam dredger appeared to the north of the chapel and it did not take the villagers long to realise the consequences to their homes and livelihoods should this rape of the seabed go unchallenged. Several Hallsanders, including William Trout, engaged in bitter arguments with the crew of the dredger, unfortunately to no avail as the extraction went relentlessly ahead. Informed that anything below high-water mark was the property of the Crown, and that Jackson had followed all the necessary procedures when making his application, the villagers seemed helpless to resist. Before long a team of dredgers armed with suction pumps was extracting enormous quantities of sand and shingle, which was then ferried to Devonport in hopper barges.

Fearful of what might happen, the villagers sought the help of their local Liberal Unionist MP, Frank Mildmay, whose family owned Flete House a few miles to the west. Another branch of this powerful family also owned Mothecombe House, with its private beach sometimes enjoyed by royalty. Although a member of the landed gentry, Mildmay was highly regarded for his social conscience and previous support of the fishermen of the South Hams. A visit to the village incensed him enough to address a parliamentary question to the president of the Board of Trade, asking him to order an inquiry into the situation.

The coastguard station above the village was chosen as the location for this inquiry in June 1897, at which representatives of the Board of Trade, the Devon Sea Fisheries Protection Committee, and Sir John Jackson Limited listened to the appeals of villagers. The fishermen, including William Trout and George Wills, locally nicknamed 'The King of Hallsands', were represented by an agent of Frank Mildmay and a solicitor from Totnes, Edward Windeatt, who pointed out that the noisy process of dredging was frightening fish out of the area. All fishermen had reported a serious decline in their catches since the dredging began. It was further pointed out that in the event of a south-easterly storm, the shingle on the beach would move into the trenches that were being created on the seabed through the dredging. This could only result in a reduction in the size of the beach, which would expose the village itself to nature's mercy. Jackson's representative refuted this, claiming that sand was already filling in their excavations, and would continue to do so.

In his book, *Hallsands: A village betrayed*, Steve Melia records the conclusion to these talks, and although the report of the inquiry, along with many earlier documents relating to Hallsands, have since disappeared from the government's files, he explains:

In July 1897 T. H. Pelham, Assistant Secretary for Fisheries, wrote to Frank Mildmay saying the Board had considered the report, concluding the operations 'will not cause any damage to the beach or houses', although he listed three concessions offered by Sir John's company. The dredging operations would move northwards, further from the village; they would stop when requested during netting; and the company would pay for any loss of crab pots or buoys. This evidently failed to convince the fishermen and negotiations continued through Mr Windeatt, resulting in a further offer of £125 a year, to which Sir John later added a 'Christmas gratuity' of £20. This amounted to £1 10s a year for each fisherman (around £100

at today's prices) and £1 2s 6d for each fisherwoman. Smaller
payments were also made to the fishermen of Beesands. Despite
their misgivings, the fishermen had little choice but to accept, so
the dredging continued through three years of uneasy truce.

However, the fears of the fishermen were soon proved founded; by
1900, the beach had become visibly narrower to those who knew it.
The pebble ridge was shifting and large rocks were being exposed
that had previously been buried in shingle. High tides were coming
closer to the houses. Cracks appeared in the walls and yards of
some of the cottages, which had to be almost continuously filled
in with cement.

A further inspection of the village arranged by Mildmay at last
concluded that the dredging was causing damage to the community.
A limitation was imposed by the Board of Trade on the amount
of shingle that could be extracted and Jackson's company was
obliged to undertake some preventative measures, which included
reinforcing the sea walls and constructing a slipway for fishing
boats. Around 1901, as the dredging appeared to continue with the
same ferocity as before despite restrictions, Jackson offered to buy
some of the cottages but at prices well below their actual value. He
was doing nobody any favours and obviously nobody accepted. In
fact, he probably wanted the houses to accommodate some of his
own workforce.

Traders who supplied the coastal communities were now
complaining to Kingsbridge Rural District Council that the road
between Hallsands and Beesands was becoming dangerous. On
agreement that the road was now dangerously close to the cliff's
edge in places, and fearful of being sued by the traders should an
accident occur, the road was moved further inland.

In the end, infuriated by Jackson's disregard, the villagers took
the law into their own hands. The fishermen began to badger the
crews of the dredgers to such an extent that they were unable to
work. Losing money, Jackson was forced into a meeting with the
fishermen which was held at Torcross in January 1902, but his
contemptible offer of insignificant compensation was unanimously
rejected. Eventually, the Board of Trade withdrew their licence and
Jackson moved his operation to pastures new.

It is estimated that around 650,000 tonnes of shingle was
removed from between Hallsands and Beesands, and although
the community could now return to some sort of normality, the

Some of the damage caused to the village and its sea defences by the storms of 1903

Photograph courtesy of Plymouth Records & Archives

The devastation that followed the great storm of 1917

Photograph courtesy of Plymouth Records & Archives

damage had been done and the village had been changed forever. The people were now living on borrowed time, as their houses were afforded little protection against future storms. In fact, they did not have long to wait, as the first major storm arrived in February 1903. On the night of 26–27 February, terrific waves burst over the sea walls, so high that seawater cascaded down through the chimneys. Inside the houses, terrified families huddled together with water rising around their feet. Doors burst open as water mixed with shingle erupted into rooms. Having stayed up all night, the villagers ventured out the following morning to inspect the damage. Part of the quay in front of the London Inn had given way, and several cottages had been undermined. But the effect of the storm continued to be felt for several days, as the quay at the southern end of the village and part of the road collapsed two days later. The winter of 1902–03 was particularly severe, as earlier gales had already caused flooding and damage to some property.

After the 1903 storm, despite the fact that several people had lost their homes the Hallsanders must have felt confident that the rest of the village could still be saved. Frank Mildmay continued to fight for his constituents, seeking compensation for those whose homes were either lost or damaged. The sea walls required strengthening as a matter of urgency and Mildmay enlisted the help of a civil engineer and geologist named Richard Hansford Worth for professional advice that would add weight to their cause. However, the combined compensation offered by the Board of Trade and Sir John Jackson Limited did not even cover the cost of repairing the sea defences. The villagers had no choice but to reject it and fight on for a better settlement, even though time was running out. Could the village withstand another severe winter?

Finally, on top of the compensation offered by Jackson and the Board of Trade, Mildmay himself guaranteed to provide a further £1,500. This enabled the required work to go ahead, but there were problems at every turn. If the village was to be saved everybody had to work together, but it seems that most parties concerned dragged their feet and, as time passed, more and more cottages began to irreparably fall away. In December 1903, another storm demolished the quay at the northern end of the village and the sea-facing walls of three cottages. The family of Robert Login lived in one of these and continued to do so for some time afterwards, even though the front of the dwelling was now open to the elements.

Situations like this illustrate clearly the desperate state that the villagers now found themselves in.

Nevertheless amidst all this uncertainty for the future, life for the villagers had to go on. When Patience Trout was 13, her father went down with a severe fever. He was already suffering from a bad cold when he chose to check his pots one morning and during the course of the trip he became soaked through by a torrential downpour. William was unable to work, but knew that if he did not the family would suffer. So in the end, one of his brothers agreed to take his boat out for him until he was well again. Whether or not his brother was entirely up to the task, it seems that Patience took the opportunity to skip school and help with the fishing. Her mother was not very happy but gave her grudging consent.

William never recovered from his illness, which the doctor diagnosed as a split lung. He occasionally tried to fish but in the end was forced to give up, leaving Patience and his brother to man the helm. At 14, Patience left school and began fishing full-time in order to help support the family. Ella was jealously determined to join them, but her mother had always imagined she would do something a little better than fishing, such as going into service at a big house. However, Ella's love of the sea was probably the greatest of any of the family, and at only 13 she eventually left school and joined the others on the boat.

Because William Trout was respected in the community as someone who had stood up against the dredgers, the two sisters were welcomed by the fishermen of Hallsands, to whom they became known as 'the maidens'. It was unprecedented for women to become fishermen, and at such tender ages it seems even more remarkable. On 15 August 1910, William Trout died and he was subsequently buried at Stokenham.

Over the next few years, storms continued to lash the village, as pockets of people clung on to the hope that the village could be saved. However, the final death knell came on the night of 26 January 1917. In the preceding week a storm had been brewing. Already the street and the ground-floor rooms of several houses had been flooded but this time the storm did not abate, and instead gained intensity. Windows and doors were shuttered; the fishermen toiled desperately to secure their boats. A high spring tide was expected around 8pm, and did not disappoint. Together with a strong south-easterly gale, the forces of nature had mixed a cocktail of destruction. Huge waves full of shingle descended on to

Patience and Ella Trout. Above: standing next to their first motor boat The Guide, *in 1919. Below: emptying a store pot, about 1930*

Photographs courtesy of Ruth and Frank Milton

the beleaguered houses. By the following morning, the village was in tatters: 24 families had been made homeless. The only properties to have survived were those on the cliff top, such as the coastguard station and the chapel. The only comfort was the fact that nobody was killed or seriously injured. In his book, Steve Melia writes:

> *At this time of their greatest need, help came from all the surrounding communities. Sea Scouts helped to salvage furniture and possessions from the ruined houses: Harris and Sons, the Kingsbridge grocers, sent four of their staff to help Mrs Mingo, owner of the ruined village shop; the Patey family, like many others, were offered accommodation on a farm, a mile or so inland; and others were taken in by relatives in Beesands and Kingsbridge, or left the area altogether.*

The wife and daughters of William Trout had already been forced to move out of the village before that fateful day in January 1917. During previous storms their cottage had taken quite a battering because of its position near the sea. They were constantly making repairs to cracks in the walls, and occasionally sweeping seawater out of the kitchen. The path outside had collapsed and they could only reach their home by walking over planks of wood that had been placed across the resulting chasm.

During this time, Patience and Ella continued to fish but they could hardly earn enough money to support the family, which meant their mother also had to rely on parish relief. Because of this, the two young ladies were always looking out for extra work to do. For instance, they would sell crabs in nearby villages or do any seasonal farm labouring jobs that were available. In 1914, Clara left school and went into domestic service, and after being persuaded by her family to do the same, Ella also went reluctantly into service for a year herself. However, she longed to get back to the sea, and the outbreak of the First World War enabled her to do just that. Many local fishermen either volunteered or were called up to serve in the Royal Navy. Fishing was an important home front occupation, so there was good money to be made and plenty of work. Ella quickly rejoined Patience and her uncle on the boat, and the family was able to slowly climb back from the brink of impoverishment.

Eventually their cottage deteriorated into such a state that they thought it would be wise to move out for a while. Their intention was always to return when they could afford to make the house livable again. In the meantime, they moved down the street to live with Uncle Bob who had a spare room after the death of his mother, Elizabeth, who had been living with him up until that point. Elizabeth was the grandmother of the Trout sisters and had been a tower of strength and support during their father's illness.

Obviously, conditions became considerably cramped at Uncle Bob's house very quickly, so when a farm labourer's cottage became available at the nearby hamlet of Bickerton the family moved out, taking their belongings and furniture with them. Eliza Anne still dreamed that one day she would return to her marital home but had resigned herself to the fact that this ambition would take some time to achieve. However, the family was never to return to Hallsands, as in January 1917 the fateful storm took its final toll. It had been brewing for days and at Bickerton the sisters could hear the howling winds as they raged along the coast and lashed rain against their windows. Then, at around midnight on 26 January, their bedraggled uncles appeared at their door seeking shelter and bringing them news of the unfolding tragedy. In their book, *Sisters Against the Sea*, the Miltons wrote:

> *Without delay Patience and Ella lit their hurricane lantern and went out into the turbulent blackness, guided by the intermittent flash of Start Point Lighthouse. Although the tide was now receding the storm had scarcely abated; the wind was howling and the sea was strewn with shattered furniture. As day dawned, the full extent of the devastation was revealed. The broken remains of the Trout's cottage at the southern end were totally inaccessible.*

The Trout's cottage was now in a state of total disrepair with only one wall remaining. Eliza's dream of returning home had been brutally shattered. At Bickerton, things were about to become difficult: three of their uncles had sought refuge in their cottage, which they naturally could not refuse, so they now found themselves more cramped than at any time while living with Uncle Bob. And with little accommodation available in the near vicinity, the likelihood of the situation easing in the future seemed remote. However, because they were already established in their new cottage, the Trout's were able to get back to work and start fishing relatively quickly after the storm. So it was not long before the tattered remains of Hallsands became the daily haunt of Patience, Ella, and her uncles. They would sit amidst the silent ruins, preparing pots and nets, and looking after their tackle. Slowly, other fishermen began to join them as they began to resettle in the area, but the life of the place had changed. No longer were the seine nets put out to sea, and no longer was there a community of people ready to haul them back to shore and celebrate the catch.

In 1922, Frank Mildmay became Lord Mildmay, when he took over the family estate at Flete House, and continued to work tirelessly for the fishermen of Hallsands. For many years after 1917, legal battles and claims for compensation were doggedly pursued, and in time a new village was built, now known as North Hallsands. From here, productive fishing continued into the 1970s, until the fishing smack from Southampton stopped coming. The old village, sometimes referred to as South Hallsands, had 37 houses, whereas the new village had just 17.

Every time a rural village was lost or abandoned it meant that an entire community of people was displaced. At Hallsands, a community had existed and developed over hundreds of years: time enough for the village to have established a true identity of its own. Many people were related to one another and adult men predominately worked in the same industry. This was their ancestral home and the home of their families and friends. So when, for whatever reason, a village had to be abandoned it brought to a tragic end a history of irreplaceable community spirit and togetherness that had been forged through successive generations. But when a village was abandoned what became of its people? Where did they go? At least from Hallsands we have some of the answers.

The Logins were one well-known and long-established family from Hallsands. Wilfred Login was born in 1925 in a row of cottages called New Houses, near the village of East Prawle. Although he was the only son of Fred and Edith Login, the couple also had six daughters. Fred himself had been born at Hallsands where he worked as a fisherman similar to both his own father and grandfather before him. "Dad had five brothers and two sisters," said Wilfred. "The brothers were all fishermen. Three of them were in the Navy during the First World War when the village was washed away."

Some of the Login family moved to Lannacombe, a tiny group of houses just to the west of Start Point, where a stream emerges from a pretty valley onto a secluded beach. Here, there were three ex-coastguard houses, one of which his grandfather bought, while two of his uncles bought the others. His father and two of his other uncles went to live in a row of 17 cottages on the seaward side of East Prawle, which was a further two miles west along the coast. This row of cottages, known as New Houses, was owned by a local farmer. It was another half a mile to the village of East Prawle itself, where there were about 40 cottages, most of which were also the property of local farmers and rented to their agricultural labourers. There were seven different farms around the village, which meant that the refugee fishermen from Hallsands had the option of either working on the land or trying their hand back at sea. The facilities at East Prawle were very favourable compared to those at Hallsands. There were two pubs, two shops, a post office, chapel and school.

Fred Login eventually went back to sea and would fish for crabs and lobsters with other members of his family from a place called Ivy Cove, which was roughly a mile and a half walk from New Houses. In time, after Fred's fishing partner was called up to serve in the Royal Navy during the Second World War, he was joined by his son Wilfred, but not before the youngster had tried his hand at farm labouring when he first left school at 14. However, his fishing career was short-lived as he was also called into the armed forces when he turned 18. Many fishermen from south Devon were sent to crew minesweepers, some of which were converted fishing trawlers. As for Fred Login himself, during the Second World War his local knowledge of Start and Lannacombe Bays was put to good use as the night-shift coastguard.

One or two other displaced families, such as the Stones, found it incredibly hard to let go of their old life. Coupled with the fact that they had nowhere else to go, they returned to the crumbling shells of their former homes where they attempted to eke out a living until alternative housing was made available. Harold Trout took his family to live in the old bakery, which at that point was one of the least-damaged properties in the village. The house had been offered to Harold by an aunt, so he and his wife, Rhoda, and their eight children managed to live there for the next three years until the sea inevitably washed them out once more. After this they took refuge in the chapel on the cliff, which had been abandoned since the collapse of the village and there they remained until some new houses were eventually built, called Fordworth Terrace at North Hallsands, and they rented one of these.

In the months that followed an interesting occurrence brought Ella Trout into the domain of being a local celebrity. On 8 September 1917, she was working out in the boat with her young cousin, Willie, when the lad pointed towards a ship that was steaming through the water ahead of them. Willie was the son of Harold and Rhoda Trout, who at that point were still living in the old bakery. As Ella was rowing the boat, she had her back to the vessel and was unable to see it, however, she certainly heard the massive explosion that followed shortly afterwards, which sent the ship to the bottom amidst a cloud of thick smoke.

The area in which the fishermen from the South Hams worked was crossed by the approaches to the naval base at Devonport. It was therefore commonplace to see ships entering or leaving the bay. Because of this, German U-boats were also known to patrol the waters off Start Point. At periscope depth, they would wait for unsuspecting victims to happen along, intent on causing as much damage and destruction as possible. On hearing the explosion, Willie and Ella immediately assumed that the ship had been struck by a torpedo launched from a submarine. However, in their book the Miltons state that the ship had actually come into contact with a mine.

Ella rowed furiously towards the point at which the ship, The *Newham*, had gone down and found one black American sailor clinging to a piece of wreckage. Ella and Willie managed to scramble the man into their boat, but afterwards found that they were unable to row back to the shore because of strong cross-currents. They began to drift helplessly further out to sea, but were luckily spotted by another fishing boat that sped to their rescue. The other boat had also gone to the assistance of the stricken ship, and had already picked up eight other survivors. This craft put the smaller fishing boat in tow until a naval patrol vessel arrived on the scene. The American sailors were transferred into the Royal Navy patrol boat and safely delivered to Dartmouth. As a result of her bravery, Ella was awarded the OBE, which was presented to her by the Lord Lieutenant of Devon, Earl Fortescue, at a ceremony on Plymouth Hoe on 18 April 1918.

Ella emerged as the most confident and capable member of the Trout family and, in effect, slowly became its head to which all business matters were referred. She had many of her father's characteristics, whereas the older Patience and their mother were far more reserved. So, as the future unfolded, and the wrangles over compensation began, it was left to Ella to fight the family's case.

After lengthy debates, the Board of Trade eventually agreed to compensate all the homeowners for the loss or damage to their property, furniture and effects. They also agreed to provide enough money to build a group of new houses in the valley behind Greenstraight beach in which to house the displaced villagers. In August 1920, it was agreed that Kingsbridge Rural District Council should erect the houses as part of an assisted housing scheme. However, the Ministry of Health suddenly withdrew its promise of financial support on the grounds that any money available at that time should first go to areas of the country in greater need. So the whole affair subsequently became dogged by setbacks and bureaucracy.

In time, and fed up with waiting, Ella persuaded the rest of the family that they would be better off claiming the compensation money and using it to build their own house. She had already picked out the ideal spot, a small piece of land belonging to local farmer Sidney Gill, which was situated right next to the coastguard station and amounted to a third of an acre. So Eliza Anne, who had her own reservations about the scheme, finally accepted the compensation money, with Uncle Bob agreeing to do the same. Ella subsequently purchased this rough piece of land in May 1922, which she and Patience immediately began to clear of blackthorns and thistles. At the same time, a second-hand wooden house came up for sale, which they bought and which the husband of one of their cousins, Charley Farr, re-erected at the bottom of the site, very close to the spring that had once provided the old village with its water. By this time, their youngest sister Edith had left school, but because she suffered with bronchial problems she remained at home instead of going into service. Edith became a very useful member of the family, looking after chickens and ducks, and carrying out many other chores. The sisters and their mother christened their new wooden home, 'The Hut'.

In the years to come, and very much driven by Ella's ambition to provide a new family home, a large house was constructed on their cliff top piece of land, overlooking the ruins of old Hallsands. In order to pay for the building of this house, Ella knew that the rest of their compensation money would not be enough. So, very much at odds with her mother, she took out a bank loan. Ella had the idea that once the house was built, they could take in summer

Hallsands today, photographed from the viewing platform. The houses in the foreground have been restored, while the dark shapes of ruined properties can still be seen against the cliffs at the back. Start Point lighthouse can be seen in the distance

visitors and this would help with the mortgage repayments. It was an ambitious plan, which eventually saw fruition, and in the succeeding years the Trout sisters ran a very successful hotel, which they named 'Prospect House'.

Eliza Anne Trout died in 1933 at the age of 70; Patience followed in 1949 aged 54; Ella in 1952 aged 55; Clara in 1964 aged 64; and finally, Edith in 1975 aged 69. Clara was the only one of the four sisters who married, but they are all buried at Stokenham. Patience and Ella are buried next to their parents at Stokenham churchyard, and Clara and Edith in an adjoining new ground.

As an island nation with a very diverse coastline, it is inevitable that the sea will constantly encroach on areas of human habitation. One of the worst sea surges in modern times happened on 31 January 1953, when 200,000 acres of eastern England were flooded and 307 people lost their lives. On that occasion, large areas of Lincolnshire and Norfolk were affected as storm winds forced the sea inland. At Salthouse in Norfolk, for instance, people were forced to flee from their homes and seek refuge on higher ground.

To see the effects of coastal erosion in progress today, perhaps one of the best examples is at Happisburgh in Norfolk. Here, the where wooden sea defences built in the 1950s began to fall away in the 1980s, and significant chunks of the sandy cliffs are continually collapsing into the sea. Several schemes have been suggested to save the village from destruction, but nothing so far has been done about it. Consequently, many homes and businesses now find themselves precariously close to the cliff edge, and every winter these cliffs disappear a little more.

Today, add global warming and the predicted rise in sea levels to the equation, and coastal erosion could be a major future threat to low lying areas of the country, such as East Anglia and parts of Somerset. It is quite probable that even without the dredging of the shingle bank, Hallsands would one day have been claimed by the sea. But when man and nature combine, as witnessed in the South Hams around the turn of the twentieth century, they can prove to be a disastrous combination.

6

OUTPOST OF AN ANCIENT WORLD

The village community that once lived on the remote islands of St Kilda present us with something of an enigma. They are recorded as having their own British style parliament, at which democratic decisions could be taken. They were also devoutly religious, to the point of banishing music and gaiety. But at the same time they are described as perpetuating a communist society where everybody enjoyed a similar standard of life, from young working males to the frail and elderly. Yet the decision to abandon their homes was made during a tea party at the home of Williamina Barclay in April 1930, a nurse who had worked among them for approximately three years.

If Mingulay felt isolated from the rest of Britain when it was evacuated in 1912, the small group of islands known as St Kilda must have seemed even more so. Adrift in the north Atlantic Ocean, the islands can be found over 100 miles west of the Scottish mainland. The biggest island is called Hirta, a name with many variants, such as Hirte and Hiort. South of Hirta is the island of Dun, to the west Soay, and to the north-east Boreray. There are also a series of spectacular rock stacks, the most famous of which named Stac an Armin and Stac Lee rise almost 200 metres out of the waves. Both of these are found near the island of Boreray.

The homes and crofts of all St Kildans were built around a bay on the south-east side of Hirta, an island measuring roughly two miles from top to bottom, and two miles from west to east. Each house was built within a narrow strip of ground, where the villagers could grow a few vegetables. The bay, known as Village Bay, must surely have been one of the most secluded outposts of British society. For although part of Scotland (and later Great

St Kildans landing stores. Hirta was not easily accessible from the sea, so before the jetty was constructed in 1902, people and goods were landed from small boats on these sloping rocks

Photograph by Cherry Kearton, reproduced from the book With Nature and a Camera by Richard Kearton, published in 1898 by Cassell and Company

Britain) and included in the official census of 1851, the islands were often overlooked by officialdom. For instance, St Kilda was never included on any electoral roll; the Inland Revenue never bothered to impose taxation on the inhabitants; and no St Kildans were ever conscripted into the armed forces at times of national emergency. The 1861 census recorded that only two islanders spoke English and both of these had been born elsewhere.

Many sources record the story of St Kilda, its people, history and evacuation, and researcher Stephen Fisk writes:

> *The social organisation of the people of St Kilda can be summed up as a form of feudal communism. It was a feudal community in the sense that the islands were the property of a wealthy landowner who lived elsewhere but for most of the history of the community had total control over the way of life of the islanders if he wished to exercise it. At the time of the evacuation the owner was Reginald MacLeod, whose main home was at Dunvegan on the Isle of Skye. He claimed that the population of St Kilda had been 'tenants of my family for a thousand years'. His claim cannot be verified, but it is quite possible that it was correct.*

One local legend told of how the islands came into the possession of the MacLeods in the first place. It was said that the MacDonalds also laid claim to them, so the issue was resolved by a boat race. It was agreed that the first team to lay a hand on St Kilda would win. As the boats approached the shoreline, the MacDonalds had forged marginally ahead, so a crewman of the MacLeods is said to have cut off one of his hands, and with the other, thrown it onto the island. However, as this legend certainly is not unique to St Kilda, it should be regarded more as myth than fact.

Although the islanders seldom met any member of the MacLeod family themselves, they paid them rent through an agent who bore the title 'steward' or 'factor'. Initially, this rent would have been paid in goods, such as the feathers and oil obtained from the masses of sea birds that lived on many Scottish archipelagoes. The oil was found in the stomachs of birds such as fulmars. They might also pay with a proportion of their limited agricultural produce, although the soil on Hirta was very poor and full of toxic chemicals. In later years the islanders began to weave tweed cloth, which might also be included. All of these goods were in turn sold by the landowner. There was no money in circulation on St Kilda until the nineteenth century.

This system worked greatly in favour of the MacLeods and although their tenants were obviously being exploited, it was in the family's interest to treat the islanders with honesty and fairness, as they were under no obligation to remain. Had they been aware of the primitiveness of their secluded existence, and their inferior standard of living compared to workers on the Scottish mainland, many might have been inclined to leave far sooner than they eventually did. So in order to perpetuate their own income, the MacLeods would supply the islanders with the things they needed but were unable to obtain locally. And if there was a poor year, the rent would be reduced accordingly.

On the subject of the island's poisoned soil, Ben Buxton notes: "It has only recently been discovered that there are high levels of lead and zinc in the formerly cultivated soil." The lead came from peat ash from domestic fires, and the zinc from the carcasses of seabirds. Both ash and birds were apparently used for fertiliser as there was very little seaweed, which is the normal fertiliser in western Scotland. "What is surprising," he continues, "is that there is no firm evidence that the soil did the St Kildans any harm! And visitors commented on the good crops."

Although many kept sheep, the main type of work undertaken by the islanders was the communal catching of sea birds. As well as the feathers and oil already mentioned, eggs would also be gathered. Similar to the Bishop's Isles, there were huge colonies of nesting birds throughout the islands and offshore stacks, such as puffins, fulmars and gannets. In order to continue this trade in eggs, the islanders would have to be responsible enough not to decimate the colonies. St Kilda was well-known for its bird life and attracted many Victorian ornithological tourists. For instance, until it became extinct in 1844, the great auk thrived on Hirta, and a native wren was found nowhere else. As egg collecting was a popular hobby among these Victorians, the islanders learned to become skilled egg blowers and when special legislation was introduced in Britain to protect sea birds, St Kilda was excluded.

Even after the Russian Revolution, St Kildan society was most likely largely ignorant of the changing face of world politics, so their own brand of communism was unquestionably of their own devising, a good example of which could be found in their working practices. At the end of a long day all the dead birds were collected

St Kildans bartering with the factor

Photograph by Cherry Kearton, reproduced from the book With Nature and a Camera
by Richard Kearton, published in 1898 by Cassell and Company

A group of St Kildan men at the foot of the cliffs on the island of Borrera (today known as Boreray), where they would go to catch birds such as puffin or gannet, or to gather eggs

Photograph by Cherry Kearton, reproduced from the book With Nature and a Camera *by Richard Kearton, published in 1898 by Cassell and Company*

together and shared out according to the size of each family. A man who might have collected 100 would receive the same number of birds as one who might have killed only 10.

St Kildan men had to acquire certain skills in order to carry out this work. These skills would have been taught to them at a very young age and included the ability to come ashore from a boat. Similar to Mingulay, Hirta was not easily accessible from the sea, although a jetty was constructed at Village Bay in 1902 in order to improve things. Before that date people had to clamber out of boats onto a piece of sloping rock. They then had to make their way to the top of the rock without slipping, sometimes handling heavy loads. Apparently, going ashore on Boreray was even more difficult, as before a sloping gangplank of ropes had been installed, men would have to leap out of their boats onto the lower section of a 15 foot cliff.

Two further skills required for this and other operations were the ability to climb up and down the often sheer cliff faces, and the ability to jump between large gaps or from cliff top to cliff top. Ropes were also used as an aid to climbing, bearing in mind that the delicate nature of some of their cargo, especially the eggs, would have to be carried with a degree of finesse.

Working in such an inhospitable environment could not have been easy, even after these skills had been mastered. Gannets favoured the towering summit of Stac Lee for making their nests, so the St Kildan men had to scale these heights in order to collect their eggs. Once gathered, they would be carried in boxes, which were strapped across their backs during the descent to the sea.

The ropes they used had to be extremely strong and reliable. They were usually made from cowhide and would undergo a strength test before being used. This test involved the rope being tied around a huge rock and then pulled by a team of men, while other community members looked on. If the rope did not break or show signs of straining it was deemed ready for use.

To make things even more awkward, gannets were often killed at night while roosting in their masses. First, the hunters had to discover and eliminate the sentinel bird to prevent them issuing a warning. This made the subsequent task of surprising the rest of the colony a little easier.

Every summer the steward would visit the island, remaining for a short period of time in order to gather and take away the goods that were owed to the MacLeods as rent. At the same time he would bring any supplies that the islanders might need. The steward was himself entitled to a certain amount of goods under the terms of an agreement he had with the landowner.

As the St Kildans rarely had any contact with the landowner, or anyone else for that matter, there would have been opportunities for the steward to exploit them. However, they did have a safeguard against this in the form of the Ground Officer. He was a member of the community who, although carrying out certain duties for the steward, was able to mediate on behalf of the islanders if they were in dispute with him. Ultimately, they also had the right to appeal to the landlord himself, but as this process involved a long and treacherous sea journey to the Isle of Skye and back in one of their small boats, it was seldom exercised.

Every morning, except on Sunday, the men of Hirta would meet to discuss any matters that might affect the village. They would discuss current issues, resolve disputes, and make decisions about the jobs that needed doing. On observing this, visitors to the islands likened these sessions to Britain's parliament. John Ross, who was a school teacher on Hirta during the 1880s, wrote: "it very much resembles our Honourable British Parliament in being able to waste any amount of precious time over a very small matter while on the other hand they can pass a Bill before it is well introduced."

From old photographs, these sessions appear to have taken place in the open air and some sources have also likened them to a form of communism in which decisions affecting the whole community were taken in a collective manner. These decisions were, however, only made by the men: women had no say in such things. But it was evidently a caring society, as the community made sure that those who were sick, disabled or elderly could live at the same standard as anyone else. They were also a law-abiding group of people, as no crimes were ever officially recorded on St Kilda. It is also noticeable from some of these photographs that many of the men wore nothing on their feet, indicating that material possessions were meagre and few. Stephen Fisk writes that:

> Observers familiar with the industrial revolution and the rise of capitalism tended to be troubled by this system. Some were inclined to describe the islanders as lazy, noticing that when there were few tasks to be done they were likely to stand around chatting to each other. Another allegation was that the system impeded individual initiative. It was reported, for

An unmarried woman from St Kilda. Richard Kearton, who visited Hirta in 1896, wrote: "The married women are distinguished from the unmarried ones by a white frill which is worn in front of the head-shawl or handkerchief and serves the part of a wedding ring, which is unknown in St Kilda." This woman has no white frill

Photograph by Cherry Kearton, reproduced from the book With Nature and a Camera
by Richard Kearton, published in 1898 by Cassell and Company

example, that one man thought it might improve his house if he put down a wooden floor in part of it, but he was soon deterred by the objections of others who argued that they had lived happily with earth floors for many centuries. It does seem to have been the case that certain types of work were neglected if they were not urgent and not seen as the responsibility of any individual resident. In particular, the maintenance of boats often left much to be desired. Boats were valuable to the people of St Kilda, not just because they were essential in providing transport to the neighbouring islands and occasionally further afield, but also because no trees grew on St Kilda and therefore the inhabitants were unable to construct boats for themselves. A specific task that was postponed much too long, was to lay a floor in the church, making use of cement transported to Hirte for that purpose and left in bags outside the church. The men failed to start work on the floor and soon afterwards were surprised to see that the 'bags of dust' had turned to stone.

The islanders had always been practicing Christians but in the early 1840s, very much guided by the hand of Neil Mackenzie the minister of the day, they chose to affiliate themselves to the Free Church of Scotland. This religious revival entailed many more hours of worship and prayer than the islanders had been hitherto accustomed. It also introduced a form of hierarchy into St Kildan society for the first time, as elders were appointed by the minister to ensure that people observed the church's code of conduct. They would also report back to him any infringements of this code.

A central feature of their new faith was the public proclamation of individual sinning, repentance and the seeking of forgiveness. Life became infinitely more sombre, as a clampdown was imposed on any activities disapproved of by the Free Church. Music and dancing, which had been enjoyed by islanders for centuries, were now forbidden, except for the singing of psalms in church. But even here no musical instruments were allowed and each psalm was announced and started with the striking of a tuning fork. On Sundays, particular card games were prohibited and conversation was restricted to subjects of suitability. Their working pattern was also affected as, for example, prayer meetings on a Wednesday evening took precedence over fishing trips. But on the positive side, the church ministers introduced education to the children of St Kilda.

For hundreds of years life had changed little on St Kilda. However, during the nineteenth century, they were receiving more and more visitors to their islands, which began to open up their eyes to the outside world and what it had to offer. These foreigners from Scotland and England, with their elegant clothes, money, and time to spend pursuing leisure activities, would have been so sophisticated in comparison to themselves that they would have felt inferior, even ignorant. From that point, perhaps the seeds of discontent had already been sown.

Most of these visitors were tourists who had an attraction to wild places, or they were interested in the colonies of sea birds. Up until now, most trading was done through the steward on behalf of the landowner but the tourists provided another outlet for their goods. Women began to weave traditional cloths and made things such as cardigans, socks and scarves. These were sold to the tourists and so for the first time the people of St Kilda came into contact with money. They began to realise that money could improve their standard of living, as they could purchase things that would make life more comfortable. No doubt they also came to understand that people with ambition or those prepared to work hard could make more money than those who did not. Individuals could therefore have aspirations above what was seen as their subservient status. The intelligent among them must surely have felt bitterness towards the centuries of exploitation. Their forebears had worked to sustain their simple lives, receiving no personal wealth or satisfaction. They had also worked to make the landlord a very wealth man. Undoubtedly their communistic tendencies were now being brought into question.

In the second half of the nineteenth century, the population of St Kilda went into rapid decline. It had always suffered from high and low points, but this was the beginning of a downward spiral. In the early eighteenth century, an epidemic of smallpox had reduced the population from 124 to around 30, but it was soon revived to around 100 again by the landlord who, no doubt encouraged by his dwindling revenue, arranged for migrants to occupy the island.

The biggest single reduction in population came in 1852, when 36 islanders joined the rush of emigrants bound for Australia. Sadly, only 16 survived the journey to Melbourne, where a suburb of the city is named after the islands today. This time, MacLeod made no attempt to replace the lost islanders, and further bouts of devastating disease and illness also took their toll. St Kilda was prone to a very high rate of infant mortality, and it seems likely that tetanus was the principle cause. One theory for this, propounded by George Gibson in 1926 in an article for the *Caledonian Medical Journal,* was that the infections were caused when the navel of the baby was anointed with fulmar oil after the umbilical cord was cut. This was common practice on Hirta, and quite probably the containers used for storing the oil were never properly washed out, let alone sterilised, so they provided breeding grounds for the tetanus bacteria.

By 1900, the subject of evacuating the islands was becoming a popular topic of conversation, especially during periods of difficulty such as the winter of 1911–12 when the weather was so bad that no ships could visit Village Bay between December and May. At times like that, things would have become quite desperate in terms of food, medicine and other essential supplies.

During the First World War, although no St Kilden men were conscripted into the armed forces, a War Signal Station was established on Hirta. This was staffed by personnel of the Royal Navy and a number of local men were employed during the building work or to help as lookouts. This contact with outsiders over several years fuelled further interest among the islanders in evacuating their homes. Then, in April 1930, after another harsh winter, Williamina Barclay invited the people of Hirta to have tea with her. Stephen Fisk explains:

> She had been working on the island as a nurse for the past three years. At that time 36 adults and children were living on Hirte, and it seems that almost all of them turned up for the tea party. During the course of the event Williamina Barclay raised the prospect of seeking evacuation, and offered to provide guidance and help. In particular she would do what she could to ensure that if a move to the mainland took place there would be adequate accommodation and paid employment.

On 10 May 1930, the people of St Kilda sent a collective letter to William Adamson, the Secretary of State for Scotland, requesting that they should be evacuated from their homes. Despite the initial reservations of some residents, every member of the community finally agreed that it would be better to leave and all adults signed the document, some merely making their mark as they were unable to read or write. The actual letter itself was written by a missionary

Abandoned homes in Main Street, St Kilda, many of which have been restored with new roofs

Photograph courtesy of Philip Hughes

who was working on the island at the time called Dugald Munro, and it was considered by several departments before the request was agreed. The Scottish Office, the Treasury, the Post Office, the Forestry Commission, and the Departments of Health, Agriculture, and Education, all became involved.

Before the islanders were evacuated their sheep were removed, the agreement being that the proceeds from their sale would offset the costs of transporting all the people and their possessions to the main-land. It would also help to pay for their resettlement. Roughly 1,200 animals were removed. The first batch were taken off on 6 August and the remainder on 28 August, aboard the SS *Dunara Castle*. The following day, the Royal Navy's HMS *Harebell* evacuated all the inhabitants of St Kilda. Apparently, before leaving they killed all their dogs by tying a stone around each of their necks and throwing them into the sea.

Thirty-six people were evacuated in total, 27 of which disembarked that evening at Lochaline in Morvern, on the west coast of Scotland, the others continuing on to Oban. The evacuation had made headline news and the press gathered at Lochaline in some numbers, having not been permitted onto Hirta.

Both work and accommodation were provided for those who resettled at Lochaline, courtesy of the Forestry Commission, but life must have been very different compared to that which they had always known. Stephen Fisk points out:

> *There were no trees on Hirte, and it was envisaged that an initial period of training would be needed. Moreover, as they had never been in a position where they had to work for someone else they had to become familiar with the requirement to follow instructions. As the families were settled a few miles from each other it was not possible for them to go on giving each other the type of social support they had enjoyed on Hirte. One or two of the women seem to have felt especially isolated, having little or no company apart from a husband who was away at work throughout the day. On the other hand, the children appear to have adapted well, being excited by the novelty of so many things not seen before.*

Those who settled at Oban were equally isolated, and some were so disappointed with their new life that they wrote letters of complaint to the Scottish Office. The idea that had been sold to them by

Williamina Barclay, of an infinitely better quality of life than the one they eked out on St Kilda, had largely been an illusion.

In one of these letters, John Gillies wrote: "This home is worse than the cattle byre I had in St Kilda. I understand from Nurse Barclay that we were to be situated in better homes, but this is worse than a dungeon hole."

The National Trust for Scotland has owned and managed St Kilda since 1956, and because of its outstanding beauty and the important natural habitats it supports, it gained World Heritage Status in 1986. In 2003, the National Trust coordinated an application to UNESCO to gain World Heritage Status for the cultural significance of St Kilda, too. The application was approved in July 2005.

The people of Dalehead. This photograph, taken by local photographer Edward Pye, possibly shows members of the Walmsley family haymaking at Black House Farm

Photograph courtesy of Pye's of Clitheroe

7

BENEATH
THE FLOOD

Although rural villages throughout history have disappeared for various reasons, towns and cities continued to grow. The country had to adapt in order to accommodate this shift in the population, and one of the most startling changes directly brought about the demise of several communities. As well as needing jobs and housing, the growing populations of major cities required services, such as electricity, sanitation, and transport. They also needed water.

In order to supply major urban populations with the water they needed, dams had to be built and entire areas of countryside had to be flooded to create reservoirs. Of course, it was not simply a question of water being needed for drinking and cooking; it was also recognised that a clean water supply could counteract the contagious diseases that often spread in urban environments. And, of course, it was a time of industrialisation, with many industries reliant on water. Consequently, damming projects affected many parts of Britain and in this chapter we look at several villages that disappeared beneath the floods of the twentieth century.

Stocks in Bowland once stood near the modern border between Lancashire and Yorkshire. Today it would be on the Lancashire side of the border, but at the time in question it was within Yorkshire. A large area of Lancashire is known as the Forest of Bowland, and at its eastern edge, just to the north of Slaidburn, you will find the large expanse of water that makes up Stocks Reservoir. This area of the Forest of Bowland, the upper Hodder valley, was known as Dalehead. The little village of Stocks in Bowland, along with other surrounding farms and cottages, were flooded between 1932 and 1933 to provide water for towns on the west coast of England, such as Blackpool and Fleetwood: an area known as the Fylde.

Dalehead was largely a farming community where surnames such as the Robinsons, Cowkings, Walmsleys and Carrs were very commonplace. The village itself was a typical Yorkshire Dales settlement, with a village green, smithy, school, parish church, post office and a public house called the Traveller's Rest, which also offered hotel accommodation to visitors. It even had its own railway siding. Mind you, at the start of the twentieth century, the only likely visitors to this rural backwater would have been the tramps and beggars that regularly passed through, or the travelling salesmen and hawkers who came to ply their wares.

Stocks in Bowland sat at the bottom of a valley, near a point where the River Hodder converged with several other rivers and streams. It was a natural catchment area, prone to flooding, as water rolled off the surrounding hills to swell the rivers. So, in the 1920s and early 1930s, a dam was built across the River Hodder and, in time, 344 acres of the valley were flooded.

The intention to drown the valley dates back to before the First World War, at which time the Fylde Water Board was already buying up land and farms in the area. In 1912, an Act had been passed through parliament, which allowed the Fylde Water Board to purchase all the land they required for a proposed reservoir. The valley's inhabitants would have had little inclination that their fate was being decided in the corridors of power. After the necessary purchasing process was complete, many of the old farm-steads were depopulated, the properties demolished, and Gisburn Forest was created from much of the remaining land as the Forestry Commission planted swathes of spruce and larch trees.

Most of the people who lived in the valley were tenant farmers, living in rented properties, so they were powerless as the Fylde Water Board purchased almost 10,000 acres of land, which included the village and around 30 farms, all for the cost of £150,000. The local people, who were used to seeing only passing tramps and travelling salesmen, must have guessed something was up, as even before 1912 surveyors and architects were evident in the landscape doing their preparatory studies. However, at this time a rumour abounded that the Army was looking into the area as the possible site of a new training camp, so the real reason was little suspected. The Water Board dealt directly with the landowners when making their compulsory purchases, and no one had the

The Traveller's Rest at Stocks in Bowland in 1906. The pub was drowned with the rest of the village, but in years of drought it occasionally reappears in the water

Photograph courtesy of Pye's of Clitheroe

Sandwiched between the chapel and a cottage, this petrol station in the village of Newton was the nearest spot to get your petrol during the 1920s and 1930s if you lived in Stocks. Mind you, not many local people had cars at that time anyway

Photograph courtesy of Pye's of Clitheroe

The Hollins cinema was a popular venue for dances. A final farmers' ball in aid of the Blackburn Infirmary was held there on 10 February 1933, after which it was demolished

Photograph copyright D.A. & C. Higham

decency to inform the ordinary folk of Dalehead what was to become of them. The First World War brought a temporary respite but by 1919 the acquisition of the valley was complete and plans for the reservoir were in full swing.

Suddenly, people still largely reliant on the horse and cart were confronted by modern machinery, massive vehicles and mechanical hardware that must have seemed like something from the pages of a science fiction novel. Also, more and more strangers were appearing in their valley: surveyors, architects, engineers, navvies and suited officials.

To the west of Stocks a shanty village was built at a place called Hollins, which comprised of numerous wooden huts with roofs made from sheets of corrugated iron. There was living accommodation for around 330 workmen and each hut had a housekeeper who was responsible for the catering and upkeep of the place. The workmen slept in cubicles similar to bunks on ships and they shared a common living room. Each hut had a garden at the front and a vegetable garden at the rear, which in their leisure time some of the workmen would look after. At the peak of its construction, the dam generated jobs for over 500 men, their standard wage being £2.25 a week.

The navvies accommodated at Hollins quickly grew a reputation for hard drinking and hard fighting. After paying for their board and lodgings, most of the workmen spent their money on local ale, though spirits were banned. If anybody got too drunk they were put in the cooler for the night, which was a converted railway wagon. They had their own canteen in which to let off steam but no doubt they sometimes ventured into local villages and towns. This situation must surely have ruffled the feathers of a few local farm labourers who were increasingly aware that these men had come to 'call time' on their traditional way of life. For the people of Stocks itself, a local drink had become a thing of the past, as the Water Board had purchased the Traveller's Rest from John Swale, and was now using it to accommodate visiting officials, engineers, and those deemed 'too posh' to suffer the hospitality of Hollins. Besides, it was now a temperance house, so I believe no alcohol was sold on the premises anyway.

The village became so well established that it fielded both a cricket team and a football team, the latter of which won the Craven League. There was even a bowling green. And the Fylde Water Board built a hospital, of which the main hall became a centre of activity for local people. There was a cinema in which silent films were shown, accompanied by a pianist, and where dances were held. One farmers' ball was attended by around 600 people. So popular were these dances and film shows that many people came from neighbouring towns and villages to attend: even travelling from Clitheroe on the train. So, Hollins was probably more advanced in terms of amenities than some of the existing villages in the valley and certainly more so than Stocks itself. A reporter for the *Blackpool Gazette* noted that, as well as the hospital and cinema already mentioned, it had electric lights, shops, a water supply, sewerage scheme, and refuse destructor.

A similar village was created during the building of Scar House Reservoir in Yorkshire's Nidderdale Valley, and others no doubt existed around other reservoir construction sites. This particular village was built in 1922 for the men who worked on Scar House, which was completed in 1937, after which it was totally dismantled. If you visit the site today you can still discover a few of the concrete foundations of buildings and see tracks from where the railway entered the village.

St James Church was at the heart of the Dalehead community. The last service took place here on 24 March 1936. Now this date might seem confusing as the flooding of the valley began as early as 1932, but evidently not all of the acquired buildings ended up under water. Walking around the surrounding area of the reservoir today, several ruined farms are still in evidence, and a picnic site now claims to being situated where the vicarage once stood. So although around 10,000 acres of land were purchased and de-populated, less than half of it was actually submerged. Even so, many of the properties above the water line were still demolished. In the case of the church, a new one was built further up the valley, paid for by the Fylde Water Board. So the surviving Dalehead community still had a church, which was consecrated by the assistant Bishop of Bradford on 30 July 1938. The original church on the road from Four Lane Ends to Bowland Knott had first been consecrated by Charles Thomas Longley on 27 October 1852. At that time Longley, who later became the Archbishop of Canterbury, was the Bishop of Ripon.

As well as displacing the people of an area, one of the more controversial aspects of creating reservoirs is the resulting obliteration of heritage and history. This can often be reflected, not only in the artefacts and fittings of the church, but by the people who are buried in the churchyard. What should be done about the bodies of deceased villagers would have been a major concern. For this purpose a new burial site was consecrated away from the reservoir by the Bishop of Bradford on 12 November 1926. Around this time the local newspaper had included a public notice stating that:

> *Notice is hereby given that under the provisions of Section 44 of the Fylde Water Board Act 1912, the Board propose to remove all remains of deceased persons interred in the Burial Ground of St James' (otherwise the Parish Church of Dalehead) in the West Riding of the County of York.*

The notice also stated that:

> *All monuments and tombstones shall at the expense of the Board be removed and re-erected at the place of re-internment or at such place within the Parish as the Bishop may direct on the application (if any) of such heir executor administrator or relative as aforesaid or by the Board.*

This macabre undertaking was reportedly carried out under the cover of darkness over a period of some three weeks, during which time 150 bodies were exhumed behind hessian screens and carried by horse and cart in new pine coffins to the new burial ground at the reconstructed, though much reduced church. I suppose this was done at night to avoid unnecessary unpleasantness for would-be onlookers. Perhaps working during the cool of the night would also have made the gruesome work more palatable.

Once this operation had been completed, the church, the vicarage and the school were all knocked down and a boardroom for Fylde Water directors was built at the southern end of the reservoir, utilising some of this redundant stonework.

The dam itself, which was designed to hold 250,000 tonnes of water, was 1,173ft long, 14ft deep and 700ft wide, and cost an estimated £3 million to build (much of the stone used to build it came from Jumbles quarry). During construction the area would have been totally unrecognisable, as huge excavators, electric cranes and massive rock drills tore the surroundings apart. An important part of building the reservoir was to build its own railway system from Tosside. In all, this meant laying over 13 miles of track at a cost to the Fylde Water Board of £90,000.

On 5 July 1932, Prince George performed the opening ceremony of Stocks Reservoir. After the Prince had made his speech and pressed a large silver button, the valves opened and the valley and village began to flood.

Photographs courtesy of Pye's of Clitheroe

In a recent article for the *Clitheroe Advertiser,* their reporter Gerald Searle noted: "However, for all this modern technology, the most labour-intensive element seems to have been 'puddling' or filling the dam's trench with clay. Puddlers stood permanently in the water that was constantly added to make it workable with spades, treading it into 'a thick and glutinous mass'."

On 5 July 1932, Prince George performed the opening ceremony of Stocks Reservoir. The future king delivered a brief speech to a crowd of roughly 1,000 people, which included dignitaries such as Lord Derby and Lord Stanley the MP for Fylde. The crowd was conspicuous though by its lack of navvies – in other words the people who had actually built the dam. Following his speech, the Prince pushed a silver button and, as hooters and whistles were blown, there was an earthquake-like rumble as the water began to pour through a valve into the valley 100ft below.

A final farmers' ball in aid of the Blackburn Infirmary was held in the Hollins cinema on 10 February 1933, which effectively brought 1,000 years of valley life to a tragic end. The cinema was demolished after the event, for which tickets indicate that the Grand Finale was a turn by A. Pinington's Full Orchestra. It is interesting to note that the tickets were available from J. Walmsley of Black House.

Black House was a farm to the south of the village on the way towards Slaidburn, so at this point the family must still have been living there. But they were certainly moved out shortly afterwards. Mr Alan Brown explains that: "My wife's late father could remember as a boy the building of the dam. His mother's family was one of many who were moved from their farms when Dalehead was flooded. They were the Walmsleys and farmed at Black House." Being outside the actual area affected by the flooding, the shell of Black House remains today.

So, gone are the farmers, their homes, history and traditions. Or are they? In years of extreme drought, as the water levels get very low, people are sometimes afforded a ghostly glimpse of some of the remains of Bowland's houses. It was reported, for instance, that the Traveller's Rest was sighted in 1976.

A number of old photographs of Stocks in Bowland and the opening of the reservoir were taken by a local photographer called Edward Pye, who had a photography business in Clitheroe. Due to this family connection, his grandson Michael has done some research into what happened in the valley, and he writes:

There is no doubt that Stocks Reservoir had to be built because of the shortage of water in the Fylde. What I do find totally obscene though is the way a whole community of people and their loved ones buried in the church cemetery were just moved out as quickly as possible with no compensation whatsoever. Afterwards the community spread all over the North, with the lucky ones still staying in the area. Something I would like to think would not happen today.

A few miles from Rochdale is the spectacular Greenbooth Reservoir, surrounded by wonderful fell country, which is today popular with hill walkers, mountain bikers, ornithologists and any other groups interested in outdoor pursuits. Down in the valley below the water line is the village of Greenbooth, from which the reservoir took its name.

Although Greenbooth sat in a rural backdrop it had an industrial feel to it. There was a carpet mill here that provided a livelihood for many of the inhabitants. It also provided a workplace for many people who travelled in each day from nearby Norden. Then, in the 1950s, the Heywood and Middleton Water Board planned a reservoir that would be completed by the early 1960s at a cost of over £2 million to supply water for theirs and other towns at the top end of Greater Manchester.

Margaret Fulwell did not actually live in the village, although she had relatives there. Her family lived on a farm on the overlooking hills, so as a girl she bore witness to the final days of this community from the safety of their elevated retreat.

"My earliest memory is going to my grandma's shop in the village of Greenbooth," she says: "I must have been only two or three years old. She retired in 1938 and went to live with her daughter. My cousin took over the running of the shop from then until 1958 when work began on turning the valley into a reservoir."

Apparently her father, William Lord, told her that the shop was started with a barrel of treacle, which her grandfather James Lord had bought to mix with cows feed for extra nourishment. But the people in the village would bring him their jars and ask her grandmother Martha to fill them up with the treacle. Margaret's own father seems to have had the same entrepreneurial instincts. When he was only 11 or 12 years old, which was around 1913, he had the brainwave of going into Rochdale late in the day when the market stallholders were closing down where he would buy

Margaret Fulwell (nee Lord) on the left, with her friend Audrey Yates enjoying a walk in 1953 as teenagers. When they were children, Greenbooth was their playing ground and they would swing on the lamp posts

Photograph courtesy of Margaret Fulwell

up the left over fruit and vegetables at very low prices. He then took these back on the tram to Norden before pushing them in his homemade hand truck the further mile to Greenbooth where he would sell them the next day to the villagers. After some time the family decided to get supplies delivered and turned a cottage into a shop which sold groceries, sweets, vegetables and soft drinks or 'pop'.

When the war came Margaret's cousin, who was now running the shop, sold few items that were rationed so "sadly there were no sweets," she reports. One rationed item he did sell was bread, which was delivered by van three times a week to the shop. "My brother Bill and I," says Margaret, "would call for the family ration on our way home from school. Two large loaves on Monday and Wednesday, then three on Friday. It was a great temptation to nibble the corner of the loaf as we climbed through the woods on our way home."

During the war years there were about 20 to 25 families in the village itself, but there was another independent terrace of houses further down the road where another 16 or so families lived. It was a safe place to spend the war and she remembers one family taking in three evacuee children from London.

Greenbooth did not have its own school, so the local children had to walk the mile to Norden each day. There were no buses or cars either, so the children went everywhere on foot or bicycle if they were really lucky. There had once been a school in the village, which Margaret's father had himself attended as a child, but it was closed long before her days of formal education began and she can only remember the old schoolhouse as being a run-down derelict building:

I didn't live in the village, but on a farm on the hills above the valley and my friend and playmate was Audrey from the next farm. We often went down to play in the village and I well remember swinging from the gas lamp and sliding fireman-style down the telegraph post. We got along well with the village children and it was great fun. After the war things did come to life a bit more as one or two families had cars and there was always a big bonfire every year with bowls of black peas for everyone. There was no electricity in Greenbooth, only gas, and everyone had a coal fire. When the village people left, they mainly went to live on new council estates in Rochdale, but some were luckier and managed to find accommodation more locally in Norden.

Before leaving the Rochdale area it is worth mentioning the Watergrove reservoir near Wardle, which was created in the 1930s. A number of hamlets were drowned here, the most substantial of which being Watergrove itself. The community here again largely worked in the textile mills or in agriculture. There was a large cotton mill in the village, a Methodist Hall, and the Orchard Inn. The reservoir was opened in 1935 but similar to other places, ghostly forms appear from the water in times of severe drought.

Back in Nidderdale it was the sprawling city of Leeds that largely siphoned the water from this beautiful expanse of moorland and hills: an area which today is designated to be of outstanding natural beauty. We have already mentioned the Scar House Reservoir, but the general area of Nidderdale encompasses many other examples, such as Angram, Leighton, Roundhill, Grimwith, Gouthwaite, Fewston and Swinsty. Just to the north of Blubberhouses on the A59 Harrogate to Skipton road, in an area called the Upper Washburn Valley, is one of the most striking lakeland settings of them all. This is Thruscross Reservoir and along the road on its western shore you will find the West End Outdoor Centre. The centre, which is conveniently placed close to the heart of the Yorkshire Dales National Park, takes its name from the little village of West End that once stood in the valley to the east.

West End, often referred to as Thruscross, was part of the ancient parish of Fewston, which also included the scattered townships of Fewston, Great Timble, and Blubberhouses, along with the hamlets of Clifton-Elsworth, Wydrah, Spinksburn and Hardisty Hill. The name Thruscross derives from the Viking settlers who populated some parts of Yorkshire. The first part of the name refers to the Norse god, Thor, while the Cross element was probably added after the settlers converted to Christianity.

In ancient times, most of the parish came under the jurisdiction of the manorial court of The Forest of Knaresborough, which was one of William the Conqueror's original royal hunting forests. Although the estate belonged to the crown, it was let out to a succession of nobles who acted as keepers of Knaresborough castle and receivers of revenue from the rents collected from tenants. Perhaps the most famous – or infamous – lord of the manor was

Hugh de Morville, who was one of the knights who murdered Thomas Beckett in 1170. Today, the ruins of the once important castle still belong to the crown as part of the Duchy of Lancaster.

Although West End (which may have got its name from being at the western extremity of the parish) was set in an extremely rural location, by the early nineteenth century – similar to Greenbooth – it must have had a certain industrial feel to it. In this part of the valley alone there were numerous mills powered by waterwheels. The area of Thruscross and West End particularly would have relied very heavily on these mills for employment. At one time there were four textile mills in West End alone, but at various times the Upper Washburn Valley could boast mills that were working corn, cotton and hemp. A group of houses near the Inn was called Ratten Row, a name which probably derived from the very unpleasant smells caused by the retting – or soaking in water – of flax and hemp.

By the turn of the twentieth century, however, most of this industry had ground to a halt and the mills had been closed, so the majority of people in West End were now working in the local farming industry again. For instance, West End Low Mill, which had been taken over in 1868 by a certain Thomas Gill in order to spin heavy yarns from hemp, was closed in 1890 when Gill's successors moved their operation to New York. So, by the time that Leeds City Council began to show an interest in this stunning Penine valley in the 1950s, the wheels of industry had quite literally stopped turning in Upper Washburn.

As an industrial village, West End might have seen better days, but for a while it still had a community significant enough to warrant its own inn, school, and church. A chapel of sorts can be traced at West End back to the 1500s, but the size and wealth of the congregation at that time did not warrant a full-time chaplain. At one time this chapel became what was known as a 'chapel-of-ease', run from Fewston, which was basically an Anglican chapel set aside for the convenience of remote parishioners. However, the situation appears to have changed completely by 1873 when the chapel was converted into the Holy Trinity church. So, once again, this points to the emergence of the village as an economically viable centre. Holy Trinity's altar was dedicated to the Reverend George Elliott, who was the vicar at West End from 1903–38.

When the valley was flooded in 1966, the church was demolished and a replacement, All Saints Church, was built on higher ground close to the western shore of the new reservoir, using stones that had been removed from one of West End's already ruined mills. Likewise, a new burial ground was consecrated and many bodies were exhumed and moved to this site, which was roughly three-quarters of a mile away from the old village. At the same time, all headstones and monuments were relocated. However, with the loss of the village, the remaining inhabitants of the valley were unable to sustain a parish church and today the replacement church itself has been converted into the outdoor centre.

West End also had a Wesleyan Methodist chapel, which was built in 1837, although a Methodist Society was known to exist in the village as early as 1763. Alternatively, there was also a Primitive Methodist chapel, which pre-dated the Wesleyan chapel, having been built in 1829. By 1839, the Primitive Methodists at West End numbered 24.

It is interesting to note here that during the previous century, when Fewston Reservoir was built, the graveyard around the parish church was closed for interments because of concerns about its proximity to the reservoir, which was completed in 1876. For future burials, a new cemetery was provided at Meagill Lane, Fewston.

The school at West End, known as Rocking School, was built in 1857 and was given to the vicar and churchwardens for the education of parish children in the three R's, as well as teaching them the Lord's Prayer, the Ten Commandments and the church catechism.

The village public house at West End was the Gate Inn, which was built in 1699. It was owned by a Mr John Peel for 45 years, before being purchased by Leeds Corporation in 1898. It was built along a well-trodden bridleway to Fountains Abbey and brewed its own ale. Here, packhorsemen could stop for a drink and have their horses shod while they waited. A hanging gate was inscribed with the following: "This gate hangs well and hinders none. Refresh and pay and travel on."

In reality, because of the decline in the textile industry in the area, the village itself had become largely deserted long before the reservoir came into being, so only a handful of families were affected by the scheme. In fact, it must have been quite a sorry sight to see how this once prosperous northern industrial centre had disintegrated into a crumbling shadow of its former self. Before the valley was flooded, the remaining villagers were re-housed and the village itself was demolished. In his book *The Lost Villages of Britain,* Richard Muir notes: "At the cost of the disruption of a few valley households, some fine monuments to industrial archeology and the beauty of a penine valley, the citizens of the teeming conurbation to the south were able to drink more deeply."

There was no concerted campaign mounted to save this decaying village, and work began on the construction of the dam and reservoir in 1961, which was completed in August 1966. It was built to hold around 1,725 million gallons of water (7,840 million litres) and has a water surface area of 142 acres. But in recent years, when the water levels have been particularly low, the foundations of some of West End's ruined houses and mills have once again been visible.

Although The Gate Inn has long since disappeared beneath the floods, one remaining property that can still offer you a glimpse into life in the valley before the reservoir is The Stonehouse Inn, Thruscross. The Stonehouse is on the eastern side of the lake, along the road from Blubberhouses to Greenhow. The Inn was initially a farmhouse, called The Stone House Farm, which was owned by a Joe Topham of Pateley Bridge and farmed for him by Will Abbott, who began to sell home-brewed ginger beer at two pence a pint. Most of Will's customers would have been farmers going to and from Greenhow to collect lime. After Abbott left, Topham applied for a beer licence and let the premises to John Helmsley, who was a local blacksmith and shopkeeper. In 1869, Jesse Peel (the brother of John Peel who was the proprietor of West End's Gate Inn) took over the licence and held it for 54 years. Peel, which was a very common surname in the area, installed a brewing plant at Stonehouse and his beer became quite famous, sold both locally on the premises and wholesale.

8

QUENCHING AN ENGLISH THIRST

As the great cities of northern England continued to grow, the need for water became more acute. It seems that water companies were often given carte blanche to purchase whatever land they required, irrespective of the people who lived there. Parliamentary Acts enabled these companies to place compulsory purchase orders on any properties within a designated area, so the people had no option but to comply. Ironically, visiting Dalehead and observing the ruined farmhouses that were never actually flooded, it becomes obvious that many people were displaced who probably did not need to lose their homes in the first place.

The authorities in Manchester set their sights on the Lake District, where there were already huge reserves of water that could be utilised if there was some way of channelling it to their city. They chose the lake at Haweswater, surrounded by beautiful agricultural land, where the Hamlet of Mardale Green and the farms around it were famous for producing butter. A dam was built across the River Lowther and in 1940 the water in the lake was raised by 96 feet, subsequently drowning Mardale Green and flooding the rich pastures that had sustained this butter production. Previously a road had run along the western shore of Haweswater and, as well as covering this and the houses, the area lost its church and a hotel. The water from the lake was then diverted south through the mountains and on towards Manchester via an aqueduct.

The need to give up your idyllic rural life to provide water for people in some distant city must have been very difficult to swallow, wherever the situation arose. But it must have been even more difficult if you were Welsh and your home was doomed in order to quench an English thirst. This is exactly what happened at

Capel Celyn. However, unlike the residents of Dalehead who were evicted in such an unscrupulous and callous fashion, the people of Capel Celyn put up such a fight that it drew nationalist support from all over the country – and beyond.

In terms of north and mid-Wales, the city in question was Liverpool, which had already been extracting water from the area since the 1890s. Before that, most of Liverpool's water had been sourced in Lancashire; however, in 1877 a report was commissioned on the Vyrnwy valley. A Parliamentary Bill next gave the relevant water corporation the authority to construct both a dam across the river and an aqueduct to ferry the water to the city. During this process the village of Llanwddyn was drowned, along with its three public houses, two chapels, shop, post office, and approximately 37 houses. The scheme also purchased about 10 outlying farms.

Today, there is a new village called Llanwddyn, which can be found at the southern end of the reservoir, just below the dam. This village was specially built to re-house the displaced people of the valley, and again – similar to Dalehead – before the church was flooded the bodies in the graveyard were exhumed and taken to a newly consecrated site at the eastern end of the dam. This work alone took more than three years to complete, during which time the churchyard and the actual floor of the church itself were dug down to a depth of seven feet. All human remains found during this excavation were gathered and removed to the new site.

The Liverpool Corporation Waterworks Act had been passed through parliament in 1880, and work began almost immediately on constructing the dam. When it was finished in November 1888 it was the largest masonry dam in Britain. Slowly, as the very last residents of the old village of Llanwddyn moved from their homes, the reservoir was formed and Welsh water began to flow along the aqueduct to Liverpool in July 1892.

The population of Liverpool and its industrial base continued to grow and inevitably further sources of water would be needed. In 1955, the Liverpool Corporation turned their attentions to the Tryweryn valley, near Bala. It appears that the Corporation, without consulting local people, had decided that the valley of the River Tryweryn was the ideal location. In 1957, the Tryweryn Bill was passed by Harold Macmillan's Conservative government. This was a private measure sponsored by Liverpool City Council, which allowed for the compulsory purchase of all the land required to

Lake Vyrnwy with the dam overflowing

Photograph courtesy of Alan Fairweather

build a reservoir. Stephen Fisk notes that according to the memoirs of Gwynfor Evans, at that time President of Plaid Cymru, "the first that the inhabitants of the valley knew about the proposals was when they read about them in the *Liverpool Daily Post.*"

Within the selected area was the small village of Capel Celyn, with its school, post office and chapel. There were also 16 farms, 12 of which would be flooded, while the other four would merely lose a proportion of their land, which collectively covered an area of 770 acres. This was a traditional Welsh farming community: it was Welsh speaking and had strong cultural traditions, particularly in the field of music. The affected farms varied in size from the 85 acres of Maesydall, occupied by I. Jones and his family, to Ty Nant, occupied by R.E. Jones, with only 2 acres. Five of the other farms were also worked by farmers with the surname of Jones. Surnames elsewhere included Evans, Edwards, Rowlands, Parry, Roberts, and Pugh. On this occasion, the Corporation was not going to win without a fight.

In 1956, even before the Bill could be passed, a group was formed to oppose the scheme called the Tryweryn Defence Committee. Many leading figures in Welsh life gave their support, including Wales's first woman Member of Parliament, Megan Lloyd George, the daughter of the former Liberal prime minister, David Lloyd George. The Committee formed branches in many parts of Wales, including one at Capel Celyn itself, while another branch was formed in Liverpool. The Defence Committee had two principal objectives, although it was also regarded as an opportunity to recruit the support of anybody claiming allegiance to the Welsh flag. It aimed to oppose the passage of the Tryweryn Bill through parliament, and to make sure that suitable protests were delivered to Liverpool City Council. But it effectively became a focus for Welsh nationalism and drew the attentions of Gwynfor Evans, president of Plaid Cymru, as the committee highlighted the growing threat to the survival of Welsh-speaking communities

The first notable protest took place in Liverpool, when Gwynfor Evans and a small group of supporters attended a meeting of Liverpool City Council. When Evans attempted to address the council at the point at which a report of the water committee was about to be discussed, the councillors in the chamber began to bang the lids of their desks in order to drown him out. Evans persisted, until eventually the police escorted him and his supporters out of the council chamber. Although they were permitted to attend a later meeting, this incident alone indicates the fact that they would face a hard struggle against such blatantly biased opposition.

In September 1956, a major 'Save Tryweryn' rally was held in Bala, which was followed in November by a march through Liverpool led by Gwynfor Evans himself. On that particular occasion the whole of Capel Celyn and the surrounding area, other than a one-month-old baby, took part in the procession. However, it was all to no avail, as Liverpool City Council was determined. Even though Evans made the suggestion that Meirionnydd County Council could build a reservoir in a more suitable location, and supply the Liverpool Corporation from there, the Act was passed. The site that he suggested, at Cwm Croes, would only have affected one farm.

Gwynfor Evans published a pamphlet around this time, which passionately illustrated Plaid Cymru's objections to the proposals. He argued that the water, which the Liverpool Corporation mainly wanted to supply industry, was Welsh water and therefore it would be far better to encourage industrial development in Wales, closer to the source of the water. Similarly, it would be wrong to allow Liverpool to profiteer from selling Welsh water to English industry. He also pointed out that if the Tryweryn project went ahead, the special character of the community of people living in the valley would be destroyed. He quoted a letter from one Gertrude Armfield who eloquently described a way of life that was still rich with local poetry and song, where recreation was organised locally in peoples' homes, as well as by the chapel and school. Evans predicted the adverse effects to a much wider area of North Wales, including a reduced flow of water in the River Conwy. Perhaps among the more pertinent points were the lack of economic benefits to the local area should the scheme go ahead, and the serious political backlash if they were to allow a local authority in England to push through a major development in Wales without even consulting the Welsh people.

Although the plight of Capel Celyn had incensed national interest and inspired the campaigning of many revered statespersons, the people of the Tryweryn valley themselves endeavoured to make their own protests on a local level. However, these did not always go according to plan, as the water committee treated them with total disregard. An example of this happened on 6 July 1956, when it was understood that the Liverpool Corporation's water committee was going to visit the valley. In preparation for this slogans were painted and placards prepared: everyone was ready for a meeting

This remarkable photograph was taken in August 1965 and shows
the old B4391 disappearing into the western end of Llyn Celyn

Photograph courtesy of E. Gammie

Police constable Gareth Owen of the Gwynedd Constabulary, visited
Capel Celyn before it was flooded. Here, he is seen here standing in
the pre-submerged valley next to a large concrete block, on top of
which are inscribed the words 'Capel Celyn Burial Ground'

Photograph courtesy of Gareth Owen

that had been scheduled for 3.30PM. However, having completed their inspection of Lake Vyrnwy, the water committee chose to ignore the protestors and instead hurried to a hotel in Bala to take tea.

Although the majority of Welsh MPs were against the passing of the Tryweryn Bill, it nevertheless went ahead. One problem at Westminster was the fact that the Minister for Welsh Affairs, Henry Brooke, was firmly behind it. Brooke, who was also Minister of Housing and Local Government, admitted that there was widespread opposition to the Bill. He also admitted to receiving protests from 95 local authorities, 210 churches, as well as trade unions, political and voluntary organisations, and some 375 individuals. But in conclusion, he nevertheless felt obliged to support the Bill, and at its second reading on 1 August 1957 it became law. Although all but one of the Welsh MPs had voted against the Bill, they had formed a minority in the overall House of Commons. Afterwards there was a great deal of resentment towards Henry Brooke, and demands that he should resign. It was also suggested that the post of Minister for Welsh Affairs should not be combined with other positions in a way that might cause a conflict of interest. But the one thing positive to emerge from this sorry affair was the widespread recognition in Wales that the country needed to become more independent. The Welsh people needed more home powers in order to prevent external bodies making decisions that would have major implications on the people of the country.

As the work on the dam went ahead it slowly became the focus of a more extreme type of protest, as on a number of occasions there were attempts to sabotage its construction. The first of these took place in September 1962 when two raiders opened the top of an oil tank on the Tryweryn dam site and released 1,000 gallons of oil. Then, perhaps the most extreme protest took place in the small hours of 10 February 1963 when a transformer supplying electricity was blown up. For this action, a young Aberystwyth student, Emyr Llewelyn Jones, was sentenced to 12 months in prison. Soon afterwards, two other men attempted to blow up a pylon carrying power cables to the dam.

But the building of the dam went ahead regardless and Llyn Celyn was formed, with an official opening ceremony taking place on 28 October 1965. A new road between Bala and Ffestiniog had to be built as well, as the existing one now lay beneath the water. At the opening ceremony several individuals wearing the uniform of the Free Wales Army (FWA) staged a noisy demonstration in front of the Lord Mayor of Liverpool. The FWA started recruiting in 1963 and their protest at the Tryweryn opening ceremony was the first time they appeared publicly in uniform. Their leader, Julian Cayo Evans, was eventually arrested along with other leaders in 1969 and sentenced to 15 months imprisonment.

"The fate of the Tryweryn valley still provokes strong feelings among the people of Wales," writes researcher Stephen Fisk. "Travelling through North Wales you will come across reminders of Tryweryn and Capel Celyn painted on bridges, large rocks, and electricity pylons. Rallies and campaigns that have other purposes related to the Welsh nationalist cause will use the name Tryweryn. In 2001 when the British Government was considering making a large financial contribution to a controversial dam in Turkey, Tryweryn was chosen as the site of a protest rally."

In October 2005, Liverpool City Council voted to publish an apology for the way in which the Tryweryn valley had been flooded, and its people treated. In regard to the burial ground at Capel Celyn, it was completely covered in concrete and the deceased were left undisturbed. At the time, Gareth Owen visited the site before it was flooded, and has a photograph of himself standing in the pre-submerged valley next to a large concrete block, on top of which are inscribed the words 'Capel Celyn Burial Ground'. Gareth was a police constable at the time stationed at Corwen, Merionethshire, in the old Gwynedd Constabulary between 1963–66. He retired in 1985 at the rank of police sergeant. "As far as I remember," he says, "the relatives were given the opportunity to leave the remains or to be buried elsewhere." He thinks that eight remains were removed and the rest were left in situ and covered in concrete. The headstones were all removed to a new garden of remembrance.

So, Stocks in Bowland, Greenbooth, West End, and Capel Celyn are just a few examples of villages that have been drowned in order to build reservoirs. But there have been others and while similar projects right up to the modern day might not have taken entire villages, they may have taken hamlets, farmsteads and cottages, and would almost certainly have meant people losing their homes. But at least in one respect their loss can be offset against the gain of many thousands in other areas who have benefited from the water their homes were sacrificed to provide.

But what of the future? As cities and towns continue to grow, often at an alarming rate, the infrastructure and services supplying these conurbations have remained largely unchanged. Often, thousands of new homes are built on the periphery of towns in massive housing developments, yet rarely is anything done to improve the services which supply them. It is therefore inevitable that new reservoirs will be needed. In the future, it is very unlikely that land would be compulsorily purchased in places like the Lake District, Yorkshire Dales National Park, or other areas of outstanding natural beauty that are protected and preserved for the nation. However, remote rural villages nestling deep in valleys all over Britain might one day find themselves in danger as our thirst for water increases.

Before and after: houses at St Eval Churchtown photographed in 1938 before their demolition, and the same spot in 1939

Photographs courtesy of Alan Plester

9

THE GATHERING STORM

So far we have established several reasons why rural villages were lost or abandoned during the twentieth century. Another major factor in this story was the march to war in the 1930s. By the middle of that decade, it was becoming clear that Nazi Germany posed a threat to the security of Europe, and it was recognised by some that in order to combat this threat it would take several years and involve almost the entire workforce of the nation. All three armed forces would have to be vastly enlarged and land would be needed for both training and operational purposes.

At first glance, the thirteenth century church of St Eval, about half way between Padstow and Newquay in Cornwall, might seem unusual, standing quite alone yet visible for miles around. Initially, you might presume it to have been a 'Black Death' casualty until you begin to observe the disused RAF runways that surround it. The impressive tower, which stands on an exposed plateau 300 feet above sea level, was built in 1727, replacing an earlier tower that had fallen into disrepair in the mid 1600s. In fact, there is evidence to suggest that the church was built on the site of a former Celtic shrine. So, by the late 1930s, this rural landscape had already been inhabited for several thousand years.

In 1938, Roy Dunstan was only 13 years old but he was well aware of both the political situation in Germany and the rumours abounding that RAF Coastal Command wanted to build an airfield in the vicinity. This airfield would provide protection for trans-Atlantic shipping in the event of war.

Roy's father, Hirah Biddick Dunstan, rented Great Trevisker, a farm of some 35 acres near the small village of St Eval, where life had to go on as normal, despite world events. It was a hard life and amidst all the intrigue and rumours, the family was brought back to reality on 4 August 1938, when lightning killed two of their horses during a bad thunderstorm.

On 22 November, all the rumours were confirmed when a gentleman called Bill Plester arrived on a Brough Superior motor-cycle, announcing that he had come to start work on levelling the land to construct the aerodrome. Mr Plester, who moved in with the family at Great Trevisker while working in the area, was the Clerk of Works for the Air Ministry. The following day he set wheels in motion by visiting nearby St Columb to seek manpower at the labour exchange and Rumford to hire lorries.

St Eval itself was a small and close-knit community, adhering to that archetypal image of an old English village. Like many villages that are scattered over a larger area, St Eval was not all in one location and again, similar to many other rural villages, the cluster of cottages and farms around the church was known as Churchtown. Little more than a hamlet, it was St Eval Churchtown where almost everybody was related to one another that was about to be obliterated. Buildings and roads can be built or demolished, but communities like this and their spirit are built over decades, even hundreds of years. Yet in one fell swoop, the government of the day was about to demolish something stronger than bricks and mortar, which could never be replaced. St Eval historian John Shapland explains:

> Churchtown describes a hamlet or village that typically surrounds a Cornish parish church. No early documentation for St Eval Churchtown exists and information can only start to be gleaned from the 1843 tithe map and the 1880 O/S map. We can assume that there was a hamlet around the church in the 1700s and we know that the cottages lay to the east of where the car park field is now located. The only buildings near the church was the poorhouse to the west of the church and the vicarage to the north. During the period 1700–1900 Churchtown consisted of a maximum of 10 dwellings and a population of 50 dropping to 40, comprising just less than 20% of the population and housing stock of the parish up until 1938.

The area of St Eval around the church was mainly comprised of small rented farms, farm workers cottages and council houses, which in due course would be completely flattened, with its people scattered all over the country. The only original building left, other than the church, was part of one farmhouse. But it was not just the buildings: even the lanes were torn up. The existing roads to St Columb, Downhill and Mawgan Porth would all disappear, with a new road being built.

"Other changes would take place as well," explained Roy Dunstan in his booklet *My Life with RAF St Eval*. For instance, the gypsies who camped on wasteland beside the road to St Columb were no longer able to do so. The lapwings, partridges and other birds which nested on Trerair and Trethewell Downs would be gone forever.

The residents of surrounding farms and buildings, such as Trevisker, although affected by the war and the building of the aerodrome, were able to remain in their homes, while Churchtown, other than the church itself which the RAF retained as their station church, was completely destroyed. Because of this, Roy Dunstan was able to record the demise of the village and at the same time witness the construction and employment of the new RAF airbase.

The levelling of Churchtown was done in several phases, but who were the people that lived in this forgotten community? Roy's Aunt Nora, who was his father's sister, and her husband Norman Bunt, lived in Rose Cottage. Norman owned a horse and cart and put it to use in the employ of the County Council. One of his jobs was to carry water for the steam roller when it was working in the area pitting. This was when a road gang would maintain the local highways by filling in potholes with tar and chippings. Norman would also sometimes fill the cart with stone chippings and pull a trolley at the back, carrying a forty-gallon drum of tar. The couple rented about eight acres of land, on which they grazed the horse and a cow. When they were forced to move, under protest, they went to live at Talskiddy near St Columb where they remained for the rest of their lives. The cottage and everything around it was levelled – even the well was filled in.

During this period of national emergency, government officials pretty much did what they wanted. In the main, the local Cornish farming community made a meagre living and was relatively poor. They certainly could not afford to buy their farms or cottages, so they were rented from wealthy landowners, the local council, or the church. Therefore, it was quite a straightforward process for the defence estate to buy up or requisition the land it needed. That is why people like Norman Bunt, although reluctant to leave their homes, had little choice in the matter.

In the two council houses at Churchtown, Sam Kent and his wife Gladys lived in one, with their daughters Joyce and Jean. Sam worked at a quarry during the summer, while in the autumn and winter he went with the threshing machine and associated equipment, owned by T.H. Sandry of Rumford. When the council evicted them, they went to Treburrick to live for several years, before finally moving out of the area altogether.

The other council house was occupied by Andrew Ellery, with his wife Doris and their son Cyril. Andrew had worked for the Rundle family at Trerair and had lived in Ivy Cottage by the church gate, before he gained employment with the Council and moved into one of the Churchtown council houses. Andrew was a lengthsman and was employed by the Council to keep the hedges and ditches of the parish neat and tidy. He had taken over this job on the retirement of his father-in-law, Fred May, who was the previous parish lengthsman. Andrew and Doris also moved to Treburrick on eviction, where they lived for a number of years before finally settling for the rest of their lives at St Columb. Their son Cyril joined the Royal Navy, and after getting married finally settled in Bournemouth.

Clarence Brewer rented Churchtown Farm, where he lived with his wife and son Rex. Clarence was Doris Ellery's cousin. He had quite a business going and before eviction held a farm sale, at which he was forced to sell off all his machinery and livestock. They went to nearby Penrose, and Clarence worked at the aerodrome for a time before renting another farm away from St Eval.

The glebe ground, owned by the church itself, was farmed by Will May, who lived in what had been a former public house before the Great War, called the Spry's Arms. He was married to Gladys and had a son and daughter, Tony and Thelma. There were also Glebe Cottages, in one of which lived Will's parents, Fred and Mary May. In the other, next door to her parents, lived Will's sister Evelyn Ball, with her husband Fred. Will was also the brother of Doris Ellery, who of course lived with her husband Andrew in one of the two council houses. After eviction from the Spry's Arms, Will and Gladys had bought a large hut that was in a meadow near the Glebe Cottages where they continued to farm for another three years until the aerodrome was further extended in 1940, and they finally moved to Trevarrian.

In June 1940, with the next phase of the airfield under construction, the glebe cottages were themselves levelled. Fred May and his family went to live at Sea View Farm with their other son, Ernest, while Fred Ball, his wife Evelyn and children Aubrey and Eileen, moved to Treburrick for a short time. From here he would trap rabbits in the winter and help on local farms in the summer. They eventually left the area and went to farm near Wadebridge.

In time, even at Great Trevisker and other surrounding farms, the aerodrome would encroach on the land. Mr Dunstan's 35 acres were eventually reduced to 10. The area lost at Trevisker included a set of farm buildings with a beautiful millpond where Roy used to go as a boy with his uncle to feed the wild fowl that nested in the undergrowth nearby. This pond was used to operate the waterwheel for milling grain for the livestock. It was the last operational waterwheel in the parish. "Sadly," he wrote, "the mill pond no longer exists. It was completely obliterated in the next decades."

It would appear that individuals commissioned by the authorities to carry out the various phases of levelling, were able to work when and where they chose. They gave little consideration to the lives of the people their work affected. One example of this was when Roy witnessed a bulldozer pushing down the hedge of one of their fields in which cattle were grazing. "My father was told that the authorities needed the land to disperse planes because of bombing," he recalls. "We had not been warned in advance and quickly had to move the cattle to other fields. More of our land was taken over, leaving us only 10 acres. Because of this we had to sell most of the remaining horses and cattle. We kept only a few young stock in the farm buildings. As there was no work at home, I went to help on other farms in the parish." Roy's dreams of one day taking over the running of Trevisker from his father had been shattered.

The levelling of St Eval Churchtown was harsh and indiscriminate, not only affecting all the buildings in the targeted area, but every standing object – manmade or natural – including trees, bushes and hedges. Similar to Clarence Brewer, with the disappearance of much of his tenure, Roy's father was also forced into holding a farm sale. Roy reflects on some of the problems faced during the levelling process:

The levelling began with men cutting all the bushes off the hedges in front of the bulldozers. Others did the burning. There were few trees to be taken down, being exposed and near the sea. There were a few ash and sycamore trees behind Spry's Arms and that was about all. I suppose my father took down all the gates and sold them in the sale. There was no point in leaving them to be burnt. There were a few granite gateposts that my father sold to farmers. I can remember Leonard Curtis from Treburrick coming up for some with a roller dray pulled by two horses. Stones were a big problem because a lot of the hedges were built of spar stone, which was a kind of stone that was common to the area. It was not quarried, it was just all over the land on the surface, and underneath the ground. It was a problem for farm machinery, especially ploughs and cultivators.

Before the airfield could be built all of the large spar stones dotted around the area would have to be cleared. Some of these weighed several hundredweight each, and in 1938 there were few options available for shifting them. To move the larger stones, sleighs were constructed using a lorry chassis and railway sleepers, pulled by a caterpillar tractor. Smaller stones were removed using horse and carts, supplied by Mr Dunstan himself and Harold Rawlings from St Mawgan. The next problem, explains Roy, was what to do with them:

At the western end of the aerodrome the land was quite marshy, so the bulldozers pushed out deep trenches and they were filled with rocks and covered over with earth. In this way they got rid of hundreds of tonnes of them. They are still a problem in the area. Even when digging graves in St Eval Churchyard they came across these stones deep down. They were used a lot for foundation stones on buildings. You can see them used for the corner stones of the foundations of St Eval Church.

The bushes and hedges were easier to deal with. These were mainly bramble, hawthorn and 'vuss', the local name for gorse. These were all burned in large piles, though apparently the Spry's Arms was also filled with bushes, enabling St Columb Fire Brigade to achieve some useful practice once they were set alight.

As a young lad, if there was any form of compensation for the loss of family, friends and prospects, it was the fact of living near a very busy airbase with all the different aircraft that came and went. New buildings quickly replaced the old cottages, until around 400 houses were built to accommodate airman at both RAF St Eval and the adjacent RAF St Mawgan. Building went on throughout the summer of 1939 and the first airman arrived in September, in time for when the first nine Avro Anson aircraft of 217 Squadron arrived on 3 October. These aircraft patrolled the sea from Lands End to Ireland, but a great deal of training was also undertaken, which would affect the community.

"One night in June 1940," states Roy, "a 19-year-old pilot was flying solo at night for the first time. He came in to land too low and struck the roof of the Glebe Cottages before crossing the road and crashing into the field. The plane did not catch fire and the pilot was not killed. My friend, Aubrey Ball, and his family were asleep in the cottages but were unhurt." On this occasion the Glebe Cottages had a narrow escape, but they would not be quite so lucky against the bulldozers.

The second half of 1940 saw the start of a 10 month period of regular bombing on the new aerodrome, reaping havoc not just on the RAF but the remnants of the local community as well. This was the reason why land at Trevisker was requisitioned to act as parking bays for aircraft, as they were vulnerable to attack whilst parked on the airfield. Roy continues to say:

As the bombing got worse, it was dangerous for the men working on the aerodrome. When the siren sounded they could be seen running across the road and down my uncle's fields at Lower Trevisker to get as far away as they could. There were not many days or nights free from bombing. On 21 August 1940 at about two o'clock in the afternoon, Harry Ball and myself were in the same field where two horses had been killed by lightning two years before. We were hand-mowing corn when we heard a terrific explosion. We looked up and saw a German bomber flying into the clouds directly above us. We ran towards the houses and could see smoke rising on the aerodrome. When the smoke cleared, we could see that one hangar had been completely destroyed, together with a number of Blenheims. As it was around lunchtime, the aircrew were having lunch in the messes, so I do not think anyone was killed.

Trevisker itself received about six bombs around the homestead but with no direct hits on the house. One bomb fell about 50 yards away and a lump of clay went through the roof and ceiling, landing in an armchair in the bedroom. Another clod went through the roof of the implement shed, damaging some machinery. There was a large duckpond on the green that was always full of water whatever the weather. One night, a bomb dropped nearby and it must have cut the spring further down because, soon after, the crater left by the bomb was full of water, but the pond had dried up. On another morning the bull's house had a big hole blown out of the wall. The bull was still inside and seemed all right. "But, as the weeks went by," recalls Roy, "he began to lose weight and the vet told us this was probably due to shock. The bull did not survive long."

The worst raid in terms of casualties happened on the night of 25 January 1941 when a landmine fell on an air-raid shelter near the hangars in which numerous personnel had sought refuge. Twenty-one bodies were recovered and one person taken to hospital died the next day.

"I don't know whether they thought it would be safe keeping the bodies in the mortuary on the aerodrome," writes Roy, "but it was decided to place the bodies into our barn at Trevisker throughout the following day. They were all placed on stretchers covered with blankets and it was a sight I shall never forget." Eleven of these casualties were buried in St Eval churchyard, a few of the others at St Columb and the rest, Roy presumes, were taken to their own communities for burial.

That night was the final straw for Roy's parents, so they all went to sleep at his sister's house in Engollan where they resolved to remain until the bombing ceased. The problem was that returning to Trevisker each morning they never knew quite what to expect. Sometimes the windows would be broken, and on one occasion they found the actual front door in the garden. For a rural family who had lived their lives peacefully down a quiet country lane, this was all very hard to come to terms with.

Sleeping away from the farm also left it vulnerable to looting and often they would return to find things had been stolen. These ranged from live poultry, to home-cured ham and bacon that had been left hanging from the kitchen ceiling. Also taken was Mr Dunstan's shotgun, which was stored on one of the beams within the farmhouse. He eventually had this returned when the airman who had stolen it had the audacity to ask Harry Ball in the cottage next door to look after it for him while he went home on leave. Harry recognised the gun immediately and returned it to its rightful owner.

In order to escape the worst of the bombing, Mr Dunstan attempted to rent other farms in the parish but was unsuccessful. Eventually, Cornwall County Council rented the family a small farm at Mitchell near Truro. "The move was a great wrench," reflects Roy:

My family had lived at Trevisker for 70 years and my father and I had both been born there. I believe the hardest task my father had was to dispose of the pony he had reared from a foal born 16 years earlier. He travelled everywhere on this pony and enjoyed riding to hounds. My uncle at Lower Trevisker moved to a farm near Wadebridge, but Harry Ball stayed on in the cottage and eventually worked for the War Agricultural Committee, which took over what was left of the Treviskers. Ironically, St Eval aerodrome was never bombed again after we moved away in September 1941.

The War Agriculture Committee utilised the remaining land at the Treviskers to grow large amounts of potatoes, and did so for the rest of the war. This crop was labour intensive, so German and Italian prisoners of war were employed and housed near St Columb. These men also worked on a number of other farms in the area.

In December 1942, Roy underwent an operation on his leg at Truro City Hospital, which resulted in an eight-month period in bed. Then, two days after Christmas 1942, his father was taken seriously ill. Mr Dunstan was rushed to hospital but died the next day. Roy's mother was therefore left to work this new farm on her own, as Roy was still recuperating. However, the family gathered around and one of Roy's uncles from St Ervan came to lend a hand, as did Ernest May from Sea View Farm, who sent his son Ronald to help.

By now, all that had been St Eval Churchtown lay within the perimeter of the new airfield, but the undertaker obtained special permission on the day of the funeral for the cortege to enter the aerodrome, so that Roy's father could be buried in St Eval churchyard. This place had been his home throughout his life.

"My mother was forced to quit the farm at Mitchell in February 1943," continues Roy. "We went to live with my uncle and aunt at Trevengenow Farm at St Ervan. I was still in bed for a further three months. The farm boundary adjoined the aerodrome. After a period of convalescence I began to work helping my uncle (who had a heart condition) and my cousin, Raymond, on the farm."

During the course of the war, St Eval proved to be a very busy airfield with no fewer than 43 RAF squadrons operating from it at some point, employing a wide variety of famous aircraft, such as Lancasters, Stirlings, Halifax, Flying Fortresses and Liberators. To accommodate these larger aircraft the runways required lengthening, which was the point when the Glebe Cottages finally bowed out, along with the last two houses near the church gates. These were Grey Cottage, the home of the Brian family, and Ivy Cottage, the home of Mr and Mrs Irwin May. A large acreage of additional land was also acquired from other farms to enable completion of the work.

Roy heard the news on the radio that the war was over and almost immediately the atmosphere around the St Eval airbase began to change, as RAF personnel wanted to return to their own homes as quickly as possible. In a matter of weeks, half the aeroplanes and their crews had gone and only a skeleton crew remained. However, unlike many other air stations built at the time, St Eval was not destined for immediate closure. Planning and construction of married quarters began and by the 1950s, when a new school and Post Office were built, it became a completely new community. Local children living in the outlying farms and cottages could attend the new school along with the children of service families.

But for Roy, if life had not already proved cruel, there was yet more tragedy to come. His mother was taken ill and died from cancer shortly after the end of hostilities. Roy remained at Engollan with his sister and brother-in-law Harry, who had just returned home after serving five years in the Army.

In the early 1960s, Roy witnessed the start of the demolition of the buildings he had seen constructed only 20 years before. "It seemed to me to be such a waste of time and money," he reflects, "that all the upheaval this caused had been for such a short time."

Today, St Eval Church stands in a remote position on a plateau overlooking the sea, where both inside and out there is much to commemorate the short period during which the RAF were in residence. For many years now, the Newquay Auto Club have used the disused runways to hold their sprint meetings, which are increasing in popularity. Cars subsequently speed along runways that had once been used by aircraft taking off on wartime missions, which themselves travelled on surfaces built over centuries-old lanes, along which horses and carts had earlier trundled.

Roy Dunstan sadly died in July 2006.

Rose Cottage at St Eval Churchtown, the home of Norman and Nora Bunt, photographed in 1938

Photograph courtesy of Alan Plester

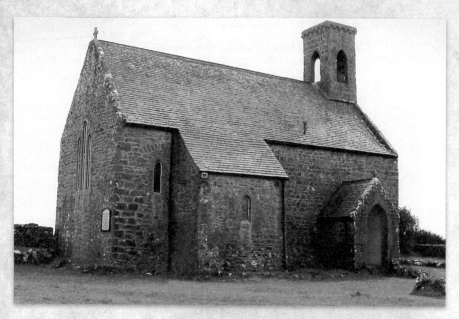

Flimston chapel is still used for occasional services, despite being the only building left with a roof in the abandoned village of Flimston. The village, close to the Pembrokeshire coast path, is now on MOD land

Photograph courtesy of Rob Farrow

10

CASUALTIES
OF WAR

During the building of RAF bases around the country, or airfields built to accommodate the 8th and 9th United States Army Air Forces after they arrived in 1942, many other people lost their land and homes as enormous areas were swallowed up, particularly in East Anglia. So in this, St Eval Churchtown would not have been unique.

In the late 1930s, the War Office Defence Estate, part of which is known today as the Army Training Estate (ATE), were also on the lookout for suitable areas in which to train soldiers, particularly where this training involved the use of long-range weapons, such as tanks and artillery.

Among the first of these was Castlemartin in Pembrokeshire, which was requisitioned from the Cawdor Estate by the War Office in 1938 in order for training to begin along the coast of south Wales in 1939. The ATE's public information leaflet on Pembrokeshire notes that the ruined buildings of 53 former farming communities that had to be relocated at the time can still be seen around the estate. The Army's estate in Pembrokeshire also includes Manorbier Range, Templeton and the Penally Training Camp, the latter of which dates from Victorian times and was first established after the Crimean War for musketry training. As for Castlemartin itself, for a short period after the Second World War it was given back to farming, but with the unexpected advent of the Korean War in 1951 the range was reactivated and has remained in use ever since.

Castlemartin is still used by regular, territorial and foreign troops, as well as by the Army Cadet Force. It is the only Army range in Britain at which armoured units can normally carry out live gunnery exercises and associated manoeuvres, with both on-land impact areas and a large offshore safety area. It covers around 5,900 acres (2,390 hectares), and as well as being used by the military, the public has access to the Pembrokeshire Coast Path when live firing is not taking place. It is also an area of Special Scientific Interest, where the Army helps to protect a range of flora and fauna, some of which have been lost in other areas because of over-farming. A few of the pre-war farm buildings are still used for military training purposes and Flimston Chapel, which is maintained to a good standard, still holds regular services and can be visited by the public. Similarly, the tiny ancient chapel at St Govan's Head is leased to the Pembrokeshire National Park.

Of course some communities, such as the farming community at Castlemartin, were so scattered that they hardly warranted the title 'village'. Having said that, if they had a church, a school and pub, they had many components of a traditional village – even though they might not have lived on each other's doorsteps. With that in mind it is important to mention Mynydd Epynt before we move on. Mynydd Epynt was not a village but a mountain in the Brecon Beacons, yet the people who lived there had everything listed above: they had the Cilieni School, the Babell Chapel and the Drover's Inn.

Mynydd Epynt, which can be found to the north of Sennybridge on the A40, was a large plateau largely covered with blanket bog and grass. Until 1940, along with a smaller mountain to the west called Mynydd Bwlch-y-groes, it was occupied by a community of farmers. The Army sought an area that could be used for artillery practice, and by 30 June 1940 they had acquired roughly 12,000 hectares of land, which would become known as the Sennybridge Training Area, normally abbreviated to SENTA. But in order to create SENTA, 219 people were required to leave their 54 homes. Researcher Stephen Fisk writes:

There is evidence that the military authorities had carried out an initial reconnaissance of Mynydd Epynt in 1912. When World War II began it was clear that the area satisfied the criteria used by the War Office for selecting land for training. Although it was home to a community of farmers it was perceived as being sparsely populated, and it did not have a major road running through it. Farmers and their families have a reputation for leading somewhat isolated lives, but there is no doubt that the people of Mynydd Epynt formed a close and cohesive social community. There were everyday informal contacts and the sharing of farm work, and in addition regular markets, the primary school, and the chapel each provided a focus for interaction. On a television programme in 1972 Annie Williams, who lived near Babell Chapel, described the Plygain, the service that took place early on Christmas morning. She would light the oil lamps and the stove in the chapel at 5 o'clock and then from the window of her home would watch people arriving for the service. Each family would be carrying a stable lamp to help them see the way. Mrs Williams was able to name the farms that each family came from. An eisteddfodau was also held at Babell Chapel, where local people competed in song; a very Welsh activity.

The community on Mynydd Epynt might well have been scattered, but it was certainly cohesive. So it came as quite a shock when on a Monday in mid September 1939 – quite literally a few days after war had been declared on Germany – an Army captain arrived among them in a Hillman Minx driven by an ATS girl, announcing that the War Office was thinking of requisitioning their mountain, under which circumstances they would all be obliged to leave their homes. He individually called at various properties spreading the bad news. However, when he attended the Cilieni School his words had little impact. This was because the children only understood Welsh and he spoke to them in English. Having said that, their teacher, Mrs Olwen Davies, understood perfectly but was so upset that she did not know how to break the news to the children. So, carrying on as normal, she left that job to their parents when they arrived home. One group of farmers was so shocked by the news that after being spoken to by the captain, none of them could speak for a while. As the prospect of losing their homes slowly began to sink in there was a sense of great distress, especially among the older residents of the mountain.

It seems that following the captain's visit, no more was heard about the scheme until early March 1940, at which time every household received a registered letter sent from the War Office informing them that they were required to leave by 30 April. Although payment of compensation for loss of properties and income would be discussed in exchange for signed requisition orders, no assistance was offered when it came to practical things, such as helping these displaced people find new homes, jobs, or schools for their children; or even assistance or advice when moving their possessions. Stephen Fisk explains:

> *After the initial reactions two things seem to have happened. On the one hand there was a great deal of uncertainty and anxiety about the future. There may have been a hope that the evictions would not in fact go ahead, as early in 1940 some farmers could still be seen with teams of horses ploughing their land. On the other hand there was a failure to mount any sort of protest against the proposals. There may have been a sense of helplessness, a feeling that in the face of the demands of the War Office no effective resistance was possible.*

Perhaps because of this sense of inevitability very little was done to help the people of Mynydd Epynt by the various bodies who had some responsibility towards them. Breconshire County Council offered little or no help, while the National Farmers Union appear to have accepted that the requisitions could not be stopped and spent their energies trying to ensure that adequate compensation was paid, both to the farmers and any other people using the common land for grazing their sheep.

The Presbyterian Church who administered Babell Chapel offered staunch support, which ultimately led to a meeting in London between church members and the Assistant Secretary of State for War, Lord Cobham. They had previously passed a motion deploring the depopulating of such a vast area, the ruin of its ancient homes, the economic loss to an industrious people and the dispersal of a community that had dwelt there since time immemorial. They also opposed the closing of community sanctuaries and the inevitable destruction of a distinctive culture. Lord Cobham, although not totally unsympathetic, stressed the point that the decision of the War Office in this instance was irreversible.

Also, the Welsh Nationalist Party, the forerunners of Plaid Cymru, added their support. The General Secretary, J. E. Jones, visited every farm under threat, and in several found people terrified of what the future had in store for them. Women in their eighties explained that they would not mind so much if they could move together to be among friends. But they were being cast out among strangers: bear in mind that very few of these people spoke English, yet they would almost certainly have to find new homes in predominantly English-speaking communities.

Eventually, Lord Cobham agreed to receive a deputation, which would urge the government to seek an alternative site, one that would not necessitate the loss of so many homes. Whereas the deputation supported the need for the Army to train in times of emergency, it saw the loss of so much important agricultural land as being counter-productive to the war effort. This deputation, as well as including Welsh Nationalist MPs, also included representatives of Breconshire County Council, the farmers themselves, and senior members of the Committee for the Defence of Welsh Culture. Again, Cobham was sympathetic, but the government's plans were too advanced. The Army was due to begin live artillery firing on their new range on 1 July 1940. Everyone had to be out of their homes by 1 June, and their livestock removed by 30 June.

So the people of Mynydd Epynt were forced to leave a life that their families had crafted over hundreds of years. Many people had to move several times before feeling settled. As for compensation, landowners received payments amounting to the value of their property, but those who did not own properties received nothing. Many of the poorest farm labouring and shepherding families lost their homes and livelihoods, and were forced to move away from their ancestral landscape without a penny to help them settle anew. Mrs Olwen Davies found a new position at a school in Llandulas, and the Reverend William Jones, the minister at Babell Chapel since 1909, took retirement

"Some of the residents attempted to maintain contact with Epynt," explains Stephen Fisk, "perhaps hoping that the war might end soon and it might be possible to return. Thomas Morgan from Glandwr used to slip back to his farm and light the fire to keep the house aired. One day he arrived to find his home in ruins. An army captain told him it had been blown up and he was not expected to come back again."

Another resident, Rhys Price, fared a little better. He would go back to tend the cemetery at the chapel to trim the hedges, cut the grass, and lay flowers on the graves. He would travel there on a bicycle, carrying a scythe and enough food to last the day. In time, the Army provided him with transport to get him to and from the site, and he continued to perform these duties until 1985, by which time he was 82. Although the graveyard still remains, the chapel itself fell into ruin and now only the foundations remain.

In the 1980s, a mock German town was built at SENTA at which British troops could train in close quarter fighting against the

Soviets, as at that time the USSR was still perceived as being the principal threat to the West. But apparently, many sheep owners, some of which are descended from the farmers who left in 1940, have grazing rights. The sheep are permitted to graze on the area during the summer, returning to their farms outside the range during the winter. These sheep can number up to 40,000 animals and as they are not excluded from the impact area, casualties often occur. However, as the farmers are aware of the risks, no compensation is made for any sheep who meet a violent end. When live firing is not taking place the public can usually drive across SENTA along the B4519, and several walks have been devised around the area.

At the start of the Second World War things did not go particularly well for the British and the initial – often disastrous – stages culminated with the evacuation of Dunkirk in May 1940. At home, military forces were still looking for suitable areas in which to train. They found such a site in the Breckland, the area that sits on the border between Norfolk and Suffolk, just to the west of Thetford. This was a massive area and the ATE East public information leaflet admits that the inhabitants of several villages were moved out. The area in question, which was cleared of its population in 1942, is today known as the Stanford Training Area. It now covers an area of 30,000 acres (12,150 hectares) and is still used all through the year, providing one of the UK's major live firing training and manoeuvre facilities. Here, all types of weaponry are used and military exercises carried out. It is so vast, in fact, that it can be used for both ground-attack exercises supported by aircraft and to practice large-scale parachute drops.

The Norfolk villages that were cleared in order to create the Stanford Training Area were Stanford, Tottington, West Tofts, Buckenham Tofts, Langford, and Sturston. Some of these hardly warranted the title village: Langford was little more than a hamlet, while Sturston was already in a state of serious decay long before the arrival of the Army. Tottington was the most substantial of all the communities in question. Today, the remains of each of these deserted villages are within the training area and there is still very little public access to them, although people can visit graveyards on application to the range officer.

The War Office began its acquisition of land in the Breckland in 1940, and in 1942 the inhabitants of these ancient villages were given one month to leave their homes so that the initial 16,000 acres could be turned into a battle area. The displaced people here were found alternative accommodation nearby at attractive rates.

By the middle of the twentieth century much of the Breckland had been forested by plantations of conifer trees. The soil was a mixture of clay and sand, and the area taken over by the Army was mainly open heathland. Little could grow here and, in truth, the depopulation of the area had already begun for other reasons. For those engaged in agriculture the main crops were rye, barley and turnips; sheep being the predominant livestock.

In his book *The Lost Villages of Britain*, first published in 1982, Richard Muir wrote:

In reality, it is unlikely that more than a small handful of survivors would still wish to return; the old villages were generally poorly served by the conveniences of modern living. The question now scarcely arises for all the villages were pulverised by shellfire in the course of the war and largely reduced to rubble. More recently a number of houses were rebuilt for use in training in house-to-house warfare while the churches remained remarkably unscathed. Though completely devoid of congregations, they are rigourously preserved, 'out-of-bounds' to troops and regularly inspected by the ecclesiastical authorities.

One resident who did wish to return was Lucilla Reeve, who later wrote a book about her experiences, entitled *Farming on a Battle Ground*. The book was first published in 1950 under the pen name of 'A Norfolk Woman'. She was born out of wedlock in 1889 at Hunstanton, but brought up by her grandparents who lived in Tottington. She was a remarkable woman for the time in which she lived, and as an unmarried career woman, rose to being the Land Agent of Lord Walsingham, whose estate owned much of the land in question.

In an article for the *Eastern Daily Press* in 1999, Keith Skipper wrote:

Agent to Lord Walsingham, owner of the Merton estate, Lucilla Reeve was plain and hard-working but not without literary talents. She wrote regularly for the Eastern Daily Press and The Farmers' Weekly and composed patriotic verses which she sent to the Royal Family. In 1938, eight farms owned by the estate

The above photograph shows part of Tottington, including Hall Farm where Raymond Pitcher (below) started work aged 14 plucking ducks

Photographs courtesy of Raymond Pitcher

had to be let. She found tenants for seven and decided to take the other on herself. She created order out of chaos, rearing pigs, sheep, cattle, goats and ducks, as well as cultivating crops and finding time to plant thousands of trees. The bombshell came on June 13, 1942. Her farm was wanted for military purposes. Everybody in that group of Breckland villages of Stanford, Tottington, Sturston, Langford and Buckenham Tofts was given notice to quit with a promise they could return after the war. A stubborn Lucilla simply refused to move. She continued to live in her house at Bagmore, but eventually the sight of tanks churning up her fields and knocking down barns and outbuildings proved too much. So she acquired three wooden chicken huts and a tin garage and set them up just outside the northern boundary of the Battle Area.

Lucilla Reeve doggedly fought on, until eventually succumbing to the effects of physical and mental strain she moved away. Then, on 30 October 1950, she committed suicide and because of this she was buried in unconsecrated ground just outside the churchyard of St Andrew's in Tottington. A few years later, after the boundary fence around the churchyard collapsed, the Army extended it, thus taking in her grave. Lucilla Reeve now rests at peace in consecrated ground among the community she so loved and fought to preserve.

Mr Raymond Pitcher grew up in Tottington in an old thatched cottage with his aunt and uncle, Mr and Mrs J. Drake. This was because his mother, Violet, had died in childbirth. He remembers a number of things about the village, including the memorial to those who died in the First World War and the shop, which doubled up as the village post office.

Their cottage was across a little wooden bridge that spanned the river, and in the meadow to its front was a natural spring. Apparently the spring never dried up and if the water pit became empty, you would immediately see the water from the spring filling it up again. Mr Pitcher would enjoy drinking the cold water by cupping his hands. He also remembers one of the village farmers keeping hundreds of ducks and geese. Every day a man would come to the spring from the farm to pump water by hand, which he would then cart down to the livestock. Each night a lorry would drive some of these birds to London after they had been killed and plucked.

When the war started, Mr Pitcher says that German aircraft would frequently fly across the Breckland on their way to bomb the many airfields that were scattered around the area, at places like Bodney, Wretton and Watton. By the end of hostilities he himself had volunteered for the RAF. However, when he first left school at 14 he went to work at Hall Farm, Tottington, where he worked as a duck plucker. In his first week he managed seven birds, which had risen to around 60 a day by the time he had entered the forces. When they were evacuated his aunt and uncle were found accommodation in the nearby village of Shropham.

Nancy Payne left West Tofts when she was only nine years old, with her mother and father, Mr and Mrs Dickinson. She remembers it being a small village, but certainly big enough to have a public house called The Three Horseshoes, a school, church and post office – the post mistress being Mrs Rands. Nancy recalls:

The church is the only building left, and each Christmas the Army invites ex-residents and their families for a carol service. The church is kept to a very high standard by the Army. On two occasions they have invited ex-residents for an open day in the summer. Coaches are provided, taking everyone to their respective villages. This is very moving for people to be standing on the ground where their houses used to be, especially as they, like my parents, were told that when the war ended they could return. But that was not so, and never will be, as it is still being used for training.

While the Dickinson's lived at West Tofts, Nancy's father actually worked as a waiter at the local Army training camp, before finding work with the Forestry Commission. They lived on the edge of the village near a meadow at Gravel Pit Cottage, which had a large garden and was close to a mere.

"Tradesmen would call," continues Nancy, "but most people would grow as much of their own food as they could. I used to cycle to the local farm for milk. The farmer's name was Mr Greenacre. Such a quiet life with no modern aids."

When the village was evacuated, Mr Dickinson was sent to Luton to do war work. As the family did not own their own house, they had to go into lodgings until a rented property became available.

Pretty much all that now remains of the lost Breckland villages are the four medieval churches rising up from the deserted landscape that were still being used for worship at the time of the evacuation. These are St Andrew's at Langford, All Saints' Stanford, St Andrew's Tottington and the church of St Mary West Tofts. Other than that, nearly every building – apart from the few converted by the Army for their own use – has disappeared, or has been reduced to a pile of rubble. Rarely can people visit the sites of these former communities, but apparently there are plaques marking the location of significant buildings, such as pubs, schools, post offices and village halls.

As a teenager, Paddy Apling used to cycle around the Tottington and West Tofts area just before the war. He also returned a few times after the war with his uncle Harry, author of the book *Norfolk Corn Windmills,* as he had an archaeologist's pass for the Stanford Training Area before the gates were permanently locked and his uncle's pass was withdrawn.

"On one occasion," he says, "I remember seeing a military convoy coming in the opposite direction, and had my heart was in my mouth. But the convoy passed us without comment. On another occasion, though, we saw a car parked at the side of the road. We looked across the breck to our right and saw a family climbing on an old tank a couple of hundred yards from the road, which had obviously been used for target practice. I thought, what idiots to ignore the signs saying something like 'There are bombs in this area which may kill you' – and was not unduly surprised to find on a later visit that the gates at West Tofts were locked. At about that time my uncle's pass was withdrawn."

11

BROKEN PROMISES

At a later stage of the Second World War, as planning began for the invasion of Normandy, several swathes of countryside were evacuated of their civilian populations to enable soldiers to train for the European battlefields, particularly in the south-west. The people normally went with the assurance that once the war was over, and the areas were no longer needed for training, the local citizens would be able to return. Many villages in south Devon, for instance, such as Slapton and Torcross, were evacuated at this point, but after the invasion the people were permitted back, although some reported damaged properties when they did. However, after the war the authorities decided to permanently retain some of this land, so the people who lived there were disappointed and, to this day, have never reoccupied their former homes.

Imber in Wiltshire, although a typical rural community of the time, was remote and somehow removed from the rest of the world. While life was similar to other rural villages in the area, its isolation would undoubtedly have produced a particularly close-knit and independent community. It is said that when the Second World War began, few people from the village had been to the cinema or seen a train: mains electricity never arrived at the village at all.

Imber was right at the heart of Salisbury Plain, ominously close to training areas that the Army had been using since before the turn of the twentieth century. Even so, the village had survived during the intense days of the First World War. But from 1942 onwards, American troops flooded into the area during Operation Bolero, the build-up for D-Day. Then, on 1 November 1943, all the inhabitants of the village were summoned to a meeting at the school at which they were informed that they had to vacate their

A view of Imber in the early twentieth century taken from the church tower, looking towards Parsonage and Tinker's Farms

Photograph courtesy of John Williams

View of Imber main street from east to west before the First World War. The row of cottages has the Imber post box let into the wall just beyond the well. From the left, the cottages were occupied by the Goddards, Edward Meaden, the Bundys and Harry Daniels. The winterbourne known as Imber Dock is shown in a dry condition through the middle of the photograph

Photograph courtesy of Rex Sawyer/Rosalind Hooper

homes by 17 December: a mere 47 days. The War Department required their village in order to train American troops in the type of street fighting they might encounter in Nazi occupied Europe.

The entire village complied and today we might wonder why they so readily agreed. But the government demanded, rather than asked, so people had no alternative but to succumb to these demands; and besides, during the years before the war, the War Department had systematically purchased every property in the village. There was also, of course, a national sense of patriotism prevalent at the time, so no doubt the villagers felt that they were doing their bit for the war effort. It would also appear that the villagers were given verbal assurances that, following the invasion, they would be able to return to their homes, and as the troops being trained at Imber were from the USA, they had little reason to suspect otherwise. Convinced therefore that their eviction would be of short duration, several people left their furniture and possessions behind.

The promise was broken and Imber was never returned to its people, today still being under the control of the Ministry of Defence. There seems to be no written evidence to prove that the Army ever made such a promise, but the people of Imber so fervently upheld this claim that plainly some verbal assurance must have been given. After the war, as the years slowly ticked away, it is evident that the villagers still clung to the hope of their eventual repatriation. For instance, the landlords of the village pub, The Bell Inn, renewed their licence doggedly for several years.

Imber itself was already in existence at the time of the Domesday Book in 1086, in which it was recorded by the name of Imemerie. At the time of the Black Death in 1348, its isolation helped to protect it and, unlike some other local communities that were devastated, its population steadily increased.

By the middle of the nineteenth century, several families had become prominent in the village, notably those who ran the larger farms. The Dean family leased Seagrams Farm, Tinker's Farm and Imber Court, the latter of which was owned by the Dean and Chapter of Salisbury Cathedral, whose commissioners would later sell it to the Holloway family in 1920. Then there were the Hoopers at Brown's Farm, which had also been a previous church property. James Hooper had purchased the farm from the church commissioners around 1904, and the family continued to farm there until the evacuation, at which time it was the home of

Captain Arthur Williams and his wife Hilda Hooper. The Frickers ran Parsonage Farm at the centre of the village, before that too was eventually taken over by the Deans. Although there were several smaller farms in and around the village, the Deans and the Hoopers provided most of the work for village folk, right up to the evacuation in 1943.

Imber Court was without question the most impressive property in the village. It had been home to the affluent Wadman family during the seventeenth and eighteenth centuries. One of them continued to haunt the house: the spectre of a female family member was observed walking with a lighted candle before her, while at the kennels the rattling of chains and howling of hunting dogs were sometimes heard. The Deans had taken residence towards the end of the eighteenth century, although for a while before they did it was employed as an academy for young gentlemen by a Mr Richard Tucker from Broadwindsor in Dorset: the academy being held in the stables. From the 1920s, after the Court was sold to the Holloway family, the estate was managed by Major Robert Whistler.

But at the turn of the twentieth century, Edward Dean was very much the lord of the manor, providing the village with employment both in farming and as members of staff up at the big house. Life at Imber Court reflected the family's social status and apparent descent from King John. There were lavish balls and tennis parties. The residents of all the big farms took an active interest in field sports and held regular shooting parties: Imber Court being known for its partridge shoots. The Deans were also responsible for arranging rabbit shoots at Ladywell Farm, where 3,000 were recorded bagged in one day. But at Brown's Farm, the Hoopers were not to be outdone and their shoots included rooks, wood pigeons, and even lapwings.

Most of Imber's inhabitants were involved with agriculture, working for one of these main farming families. There were two types of farming in the area: arable and sheep. In the sheltered valley, crops such as kale, rape, swedes and turnips could be grown. A lot of corn was also harvested in the larger fields. Strip lynchets all over Salisbury Plain indicate that arable farming was an ancient activity throughout the area. But the sheep, mainly Hampshire Down sheep, which were well suited to the surrounding chalk downland, were the lifeblood of the community.

Shepherding was a full-time specialist occupation, which entailed long working hours, both day and night. Wages reflected this

Occasionally evangelical groups would come to preach the gospel like this one led by Mr and Mrs Ware around 1909. There is a text-covered van in front of the tent, domestic servants to the right from Imber Court (which can be seen in the background) and shepherds returning from the downs behind them. The event continued for about two weeks – much to the displeasure of the vicar

Photograph courtesy of Rex Sawyer/Rosalind Hooper

The beautiful Imber Court photographed before the fire. The Dean family leased it from the Dean and Chapter of Salisbury Cathedral before it was sold to the Holloway family in 1920

Photograph courtesy of Ken Mitchell

The Reverend James Hugh Pearson, vicar of Imber from 1885–99
with his housekeeper, Mrs Payton, and the 'garden' boy

Photograph courtesy of Rex Sawyer/Rosalind Hooper

This turn of the twentieth century picture was taken when the
blacksmith's shop was a lean-to on the side of Granny Staples
house. The man shoeing the horse is probably James Staples, the
village blacksmith before Albert Nash (who is holding the toolbox)

Photograph courtesy of Ken Mitchell

and shepherds were paid a better rate than other farm labourers. A shepherd's cottage was his workplace as well as his home. In the lambing season, the cottage stove would be kept going all night, while the shepherd scoured the downs with a lantern, looking for chilled or ailing lambs which would then be taken home to warm and revive.

Shepherds also had a mobile home, a timber-framed shed mounted on wheels faced with corrugated iron sheeting. These sheds, which were drawn to locations near the pens by horses, were built at the iron works at Bratton. One Imber shepherd, Thomas Carter, who worked in the area during the early twentieth century, described them as having sparse interiors, containing little more than a stove for cooking and for heating milk for the sickly lambs. His bed was usually made of straw bales. While working from such mobile homes in remote quarters of the downs, the lambs and their faithful sheepdogs would have been the shepherd's only companions. Still, this was an improvement from the conditions enjoyed by Mr Carter's grandfather, who spent such nights protected by a simple shelter formed by thatching a couple of sheep hurdles together. Salisbury Plain presented a cruel and treacherous environment, occasionally even fatal to those lost or ill-prepared to deal with its harshness. The shepherd would also be responsible for driving the flocks to sheep fairs or midsummer shearings nearer the village.

Most other farming operations still employed teams of horses, as the first tractors did not arrive in the village until after the First World War. Fields were ploughed using a team of two horses and corn would be ferried to Warminster aboard a farmer's horse drawn wagon. But even the arable farmer depended on sheep, as before the arrival of artificial manures their droppings were used to fertilise the fields.

As for life in the village itself, a post office opened in 1909, run by Ellen and John Carter from then until its subsequent closure in 1943. The Carters were the first people in the village to own a telephone, and John was also the carpenter, with his premises adjacent to the post office. Previously the postman had daily walked or cycled from the village of Codford, a journey of some seven miles. The mail collection point before the arrival of the post office was a village letterbox situated in the High Street. Having delivered the mail at 9 AM, the postman would then spend the rest of the day at the village, either sheltering in a special tin hut or by performing odd jobs for people. He would then return to Codford at around 4.20 PM with the outgoing mail. Early doctors to serve the community would also walk from Codford, although at least one was known to have a gig.

Water was always a bit of a problem in the village. There was an unreliable watercourse known as Imber Dock that ran through its centre. During the wet months of winter, rainfall on the downs would cause the river to swell and often flood the street, while during the summer it would completely dry up. When this happened the only other available water came from two wells, one on land belonging to Sydney Dean, and the other at Imber Court. Consequently, every house in the village had an array of buckets and barrels in an attempt to catch rainwater.

During the inter-war years, a bus linking Warminster to Devizes would pass through Imber once a week, and a return journey was possible to either town on the day in question. And once a year, the entire village – or at least those who were interested – would enjoy a charabanc outing to a seaside town, such as Weston-super-Mare or Bournemouth. The village's main sport was cricket, played on an area set aside for recreational purposes called the Barley Field, and villagers would go to the The Bell Inn to socialize, which had a small shop at the rear where people could buy groceries and confectionery.

So by 1943, although isolated and perhaps even more close-knit than neighbouring villages, Imber had evolved into a typical rural community, complete with post office, church, chapel and pub. Ken Mitchell was born at Imber in 1926 where his grandfather Albert Nash – known locally as 'Albie' – had been the village blacksmith for over 40 years. Albert was married to Martha and descended from a long line of Imber shepherds. Ken's father was Frederick Mitchell and his mother was Albert's daughter, Gladys. He also had a brother and sister, Derrick and Doreen. They were a close family who would enjoy evening walks together in the summer sunshine; or they would sit together in the garden, the children drinking lemonade and the adults something a little stronger.

Albert Nash was a very respected member of the community and in a time when horses still did the majority of heavy work on local farms, he provided a very important service. He was a prize-winning farrier, known at many agricultural shows, but he would also repair farm machinery and bicycles, and manufacture any special tools needed by farmers, shepherds and other local craftsmen. He also kept a few beehives and made his own mead, a favourite beverage at Christmas. Ken Mitchell explains:

> *My birthplace was a traditional thatched cottage in an area known as the Barracks, situated to the rear of the blacksmith shop. The fact we lived so near his workplace meant that from an early age I was closely associated with grandfather and the blacksmith shop. It must have been comforting for mother to know her father was close at hand, if needed, particularly later on when brother Derrick and sister Doreen came along. She must have had her hands full, when you consider every drop of water used in the home had to be drawn from a well about two hundred yards away. In summer the water level would drop considerably, which made winding a bucket to the surface very hard work. When the three of us were eventually at school mother started to work part-time for the Whistler family at Imber Court. One of her duties was the weekly laundry, and once again mother had to do it the hard way. It was a long walk to the clothesline, which was about four hundred yards uphill: a good place for a washing line, but hard on dear mum. Every week that household produced a lot of washing! In those days you had to work for your money!*

Another of Albert's skills as a blacksmith was the art of bonding cartwheels, which basically meant putting a metal strip around a wooden wheel to protect it: similar to a modern tyre. There were many occasions when the young Ken helped his grandfather in this task. "As a youngster," he states, "I would be standing by, usually with another person, both of us with a garden watering can filled with water. When the almost red hot iron bond was in place, on the word from Albert we would apply the water to the bond to prevent it from burning the wooden wheel. At the same time the cooling effect on the metal bond caused it to contract, thereby holding it firmly in place."

Although Ken lived near the smithy, his grandparents lived about a quarter of a mile away. The house had a large garden extending to the back of The Bell Inn, which was very convenient on summer evenings "as there was a window in the bar that could be used as a serving hatch."

Albert also had another large garden at the smithy, where he grew vegetables. He also planted numerous fruit trees, and Ken remembers that his Beauty of Bath apples were delicious! He grew flowers, including dahlias and chrysanthemums. Ken recalls that his flowers were considered to be of show standard, but Imber had no flower show in which to present them. He then goes on to confirm:

Where Albert did achieve considerable success was at the big agricultural shows with his skill in horseshoe making, winning many awards over the years. In the winter when life slowed down in the countryside he kept himself busy catching rabbits for farmers Dean and Hooper. Keeping the rabbit population under control in wartime was essential for the protection of crops, and of course the rabbits were valued as food. In a shed at the back of the forge, ferrets were kept. These were used to drive the rabbits from their burrows to be caught in nets placed over the holes. Bee keeping was another pastime of his. After extracting the honey, he would use the comb to make mead. He also made wine with fruit or vegetables from the garden. Albert liked to drink his mead or wine, mulled, during the wintertime. Although it was a long time ago, I can still picture him now, sitting by an open fire with glass in hand and a little saucepan of wine just close enough to the fire to take the chill off. At Christmas time, when he would be joined by family and friends, the saucepan was replaced with another one, somewhat bigger.

Just before the start of the war Albert, Martha, and their son Cyril moved into a newly built house, which proved to be a great improvement on the old one. "Martha was really pleased with her new home," explains Ken. "It was so much bigger, with three bedrooms. At last she lived in a home with some space." Unfortunately, it was not to last. When the war started, because they had a spare bedroom, Martha was asked to take in evacuees. She agreed to accept a mother with two children from London. Many problems were encountered, as one would expect, making life difficult, but Martha dealt with it in a sympathetic and kindly way, thereby "avoiding a lot of unpleasantness."

Another person whose memories capture Imber exactly as it was in 1943 – and for very good reason – is John Williams. As a seven-year-old he had accompanied his mother, Myfanwy Williams, to Imber on her appointment as the new schoolmistress. His father

Bonding a cartwheel in front of the Imber blacksmith shop.
From left to right: Harry Marsh, Dollie Coleman (or Flossie Nash),
Billie Burgess, Edward Marsh, Edward Pearce, Frank Carpenter
and Albie

Photograph courtesy of Ken Mitchell

was away working for the Air Ministry. Little did they know that within months they would be returning back to North Wales again, due to the evacuation of the village. As a seven-year-old the events of those few months have left a lasting impression and his boyhood memories of the village are still very vivid:

Well, I remember the train journey from Caernarvon (it was spelt with a 'v' in those days), through the Severn Tunnel – changing trains at Bristol and arriving at Warminster station. After that, being driven out of Warminster up the Imber Road and onto Salisbury Plain, passing red brick houses that are still there today. The army garrison and the married quarters that now straddle the road were not built then. I well recall my mother asking how far it was to Imber, and the driver reciting the couplet in reply! 'Little Imber on the Downe... Seven miles from any towne'. Approaching from that direction, Imber cannot be seen until you suddenly drop down into the trees, and round the corner there it is. We were dropped at the post office and directed to our lodgings – that being the word used in those days. We were staying in the third house in a block of four, which had been built just before the start of the war. It was very new with mod cons, compared with the rest of the houses in the village that were typical of a rural and rustic village of the time, many still thatched. By mod cons I mean a bathroom. I think the WC was outside in an adjoining building? I don't remember electricity and the public phone was in the post office.

John remembers life being quiet and undisturbed. He also recalls that everyone respected each other and knew their place. As a child, he knew it was wrong to trespass in the grounds of Imber Court, for instance. On most Saturdays his mother took him to Warminster on the bus, a normal part of village routine for many people. The bus stop was near Seagrams Farm, which John describes as "another 'tidy' farmhouse that saw itself as a cut above the rest!"

John also recalls that the stream known as Imber Dock, which ran along the main street of the village, was at that time in the process of being diverted into large concrete pipes. The idea being to bury the stream in order to widen the road to accommodate the increasing military traffic that passed through on its was on to Salisbury Plain for training purposes. "The dare for us children," he says, "was to crawl through these pipes, get covered in mud and face a telling off! Well, I was only seven at the time."

Sometimes he accompanied his mother to the vicarage for tea, dressed in his Sunday best. This was a large "palatial house" with well-manicured gardens that he would look out on and admire whilst his mother and the rector were deep in conversation.

Ken Mitchell also has reason to remember the vicarage, as his father had worked there for a time:

My father 'Fred', as he was known to the villagers, was born in Bishopstone near Salisbury. On moving into the village he was taken on as gardener for the vicar of Imber the Reverend Walser. He was not only the gardener but a friend to the vicar, who lived alone in the large stately vicarage that stood in about an acre of gardens. Besides looking after these gardens, part of his time was spent working inside the vicarage carrying out various household chores. Most evenings he would go back to check that everything was all in order, before the vicar settled down for the night.

Ken's mother, Gladys, sometimes helped around St Giles Church, as her mother, Martha, was one of the caretakers and cleaners. He recalls that during the winter a huge coke burning stove was used to heat the building: "I would help by carrying fuel that was stored to the rear of the Church, then clear away the ash, and lay the kindling wood ready for the next service. When I was old enough I was allowed to light up on Saturday afternoon, and then go back to stoke up in the evening. I liked to do this before dark, as the only lighting in the Church was by oil lamps."

Soon after the war started, things changed slightly for Ken and his family. Because of government regulations his father was no longer allowed to work at the vicarage and was directed to work on the land instead. He went to work for Major Whistler at Imber Court, but this was unfortunate for his family because up until that point they had been living in a newer house owned by one of the other farmers in the village, Sydney Dean. However, because he chose to work at Imber Court, Sydney Dean gave them notice to get out. "Unfortunately for us," Ken recalls, "this meant we had to move back into an older dwelling again. It didn't go down well, because we had become accustomed to hot and cold running water with a bath, which was a luxury in Imber."

Ken attended the village school in the days before Mrs Williams had taken over the helm. His teacher then was Miss Miles, who he remembers being strict but fair. As a general rule, children were well behaved and the only times she really got angry was when a convoy of tanks trundled through the village, as the children were unable to concentrate. If tanks appeared during their lunch break, the children would invariably arrive late for the afternoon session. This would frustrate her, because she was unable to keep the children behind after school to catch up with lost lessons. She lived in Warminster and when the older children were dropped off by taxi at the end of the day, it would then have to ferry her back to town.

Similar to many schoolboys when not at school, Ken was doing odd jobs to earn a little pocket money. His first job, straight after lessons had finished, was to collect the milk cans belonging to Mrs Carter at the post office and one or two other households, which he would then take up to Imber Court to be filled with milk. Mrs Carter paid him six pence a week for providing this service. In the summer, during haymaking and harvesting, after he had finished his milk round he would go to his grandmother's house to collect the tea things she had prepared for his Uncle Cyril, who would be working somewhere out in the fields. Having found him, they would then sit down together and enjoy the meal. This would include sandwiches filled with homemade jam and cake that grandma had made herself. Tea would be poured from a bottle that had been placed in a thick sock to keep it warm.

When he was 11, Ken moved on to Sambourne School in Warminster, which he enjoyed, but each day during his lunch break he would visit the town to buy odds and ends for the people at home. These might include screws or small nuts and bolts, bought from the ironmonger's for his grandfather. He left school at 14 in December 1940 and went to work with Albert, helping around the smithy or with his rabbit catching. Ken explains:

At the end of April when the rabbit season ended, there was not enough work to support the two of us, so I moved on to Imber Court, working in and around the house. One of my duties was to do the milking, take it to the scullery in the big house, and put it through the cooler. It was then ready to be measured into the milk cans of the people waiting at the door. After a few lessons I was able to take over. Only four or five cows were kept in milk to supply the house, the workers, and one or two others in the village. The farm's main herd were beef cattle that roamed on the Plain.

Naturally, Ken also remembers the many social and sporting activities that went on in the village before the war:

During the summer when not in school, the youngsters were to be seen on the Barley Ground playing cricket. There were two pitches, one for the grown-ups where serious games were played, and another for the boys who used to practice most of their spare time, so that one day they would be good enough to become a member of the village team. Considering the size of the village, Imber had a really good side, winning a fair proportion of matches, particularly on their own pitch.

A number of social events were organised by the Whistler Family at Imber Court, one of which was the annual rook shoot that took place in the late spring before the trees were in full leaf, and the young birds were about to leave the nest. "To me it was cruel to shoot them before they could even fly," writes Ken, "but if it had to be carried out to protect the crops maybe it was justified. It was traditional the next day, to sort out the young rooks from the old, and distribute them around the village to anyone who would like them; most people were pleased to accept them to make a rook pie."

So life happily carried on at Imber as the village joined in with national high days and holidays. These included the Coronation of George VI in 1937, when celebrations were held at Imber Court. King George V's Jubilee celebrations fell foul of an unforeseen danger, when a burning tar barrel rolled down the side of the hill towards the village, much to the alarm of the waiting spectators. The barrel had been placed on top of a tripod that stood over the Jubilee bonfire. The idea was that the burning pitch would drip down on to the fire. However, the tripod supports burnt through, which sent the barrel cascading down on to the Barley Field below.

There were very few areas of southern England that the Army could use to support training with modern weapons, such as tanks and long-range artillery, so the vast and largely uninhabited expanses of Salisbury Plain seemed ideal. By 1902, the War Office had already acquired around 40,000 acres of land on the eastern side of the Plain. By this time, military vehicles and soldiers in general were becoming increasingly visible in the surrounding landscape. The outbreak of the First World War would have a considerable impact on the village.

In 1914, Salisbury Plain became one of the most important training centres in the country, as thousands of troops began to arrive. Then, in 1916, an artillery school was established on Chapperton Down, between Imber and Tilshead.

Soldiers were billeted at Imber Court, with 46 other ranks accommodated in the attic, while their six officers enjoyed some of the more comfortable accommodation provided by the house itself. Edward Dean had died in 1910 and the Court was now under the charge of his son Tom, who was himself away serving in the Army. Tom's sister, Gladys, and one of the maids would provide tea for the soldiers every morning before their departure at 6AM. To help with the morale of these and other visiting troops, concerts were staged in the great barn, at which Gladys would accompany the men on the piano, as they sang popular and patriotic songs of the day.

Much to its credit, the entire village rallied around, opening their doors and extending what hospitality they could, even though their lives must have been severely disrupted. At times they became virtual prisoners, only permitted to leave the village three times a week to visit Warminster for shopping. Several houses were damaged by shellfire, so when the war eventually ended the people must have breathed a collective sigh of relief.

While all of this was going on, several men from the village had been off fighting in the war themselves. In 1920, a memorial was erected in their honour along the High Street in front of Albert Nash's blacksmith shop. It was erected on land given by James Hooper from Brown's Farm. This modest wooden cross was dedicated to the memory of the three servicemen from Imber who had died – Ernest Marsh and Harold Kitley, both killed in France; and Arthur Norris who died at Gallipoli. Also listed were the names of all those who had served in the armed forces. In 1993, to mark the fiftieth anniversary of the village's evacuation, the cross was renovated and placed on a wall in St Giles Church.

After the war, the village resumed its agricultural life. However, a major change occurred when the ecclesiastical commissioners sold Imber Court to the Holloways in 1920. The Holloways were a wealthy family from the Lavington Estate, who had gained their fortune from running a successful building firm in London. During renovations after the purchase, Imber Court was dramatically destroyed by fire, which was believed to have been started by a workman's torch. The Holloways had no intention of living at the Court themselves, it was merely a financial investment, and following its reconstruction the estate was managed by retired army major, Robert Whistler. Although mains electricity never reached the village, Imber Court now boasted a generator that provided it with its own source of power.

After the sale of the Court, Tom Dean moved away from Imber, but Sydney Dean continued to farm the land at Seagrams, Tinker's and Parsonage Farms, while the Hoopers were still in residence at Brown's Farm. But this was a difficult time for farming communities, as during the 1920s and 1930s there was an agricultural depression, with low prices being paid for grain, wool, or mutton, all of which sustained Imber's traditional economy. As large-scale vegetable cultivation was impossible, due to the area's unpredictable weather and remoteness from markets, some of the farmers experimented with cattle. However, cattle proved unsuitable for the downs, so little could be done to prevent the overall decline in land prices.

By the late 1920s, the War Office was showing an increased determination to purchase more land on Salisbury Plain to the west of Devizes. They began to approach the local landowners, with offers that were difficult to ignore. In his book, *Little Imber on the Down*, Rex Sawyer writes:

> *The tenancy agreements offered to the Imber farmers varied but were generally considered quite reasonable. The Hoopers at Brown's Farm, for example, were offered £20 an acre. Stock-proof fencing, gates and other maintenance work were also financed by taxpayers' money. The land was divided into two sections: Schedule i and Schedule iii. Schedule i land was rented at ten shillings an acre per annum to the farmer and compensation given for any damage done by the army. Schedule iii land was rented at two shillings and six pence per acre but with no compensation in the event of damage. As a general rule areas under crops before a military exercise, were Schedule iii.*

Bargaining for land was done on an individual basis and under the agreements offered by the War Office, if a farmer sold his land it would be rented back to him at a very favourable rate. It was indicated that during peacetime the land would only be required for a couple of weeks a year to accommodate a two-week annual exercise, which would only take place after the local harvest had been yielded. It was also feared that although sales were voluntary, if it eventually came to compulsory purchase the price paid would be much lower.

"By 1932, therefore," wrote Rex Sawyer, "with naïve unawareness of events to come, the farmers had relinquished the whole of the village to the War Department with the exception of the chapel, the Bell Inn, and the property (the church, vicarage and school) under the control of the church commissioners."

In 1938, the Army rehoused some of the village folk when they demolished a group of mud-walled cottages that lined the High Street and employed a firm of builders from Radstock to replace them with new, inexpensive housing. Although basic and still having outside bucket lavatories, they at least had hot and cold running water and a bath.

Once again the outbreak of war in 1939 would have immediate effect on the village as military activity increased on the Plain. Several men departed on military service. Food production was increased in the valley with prisoners of war being sent to help with the harvest in 1940, and batches of evacuees arriving to escape the London bombing. Mind you, for a tiny village, Imber witnessed its fair share of air activity and was bombed several times, as the Germans were well aware of Salisbury Plain's military significance. There was a company of Local Defence Volunteers, commanded by Captain Arthur Williams, who lived at Brown's Farm and was married to Hilda Hooper. During the First World War, Arthur Williams had himself served on the Imber gunnery ranges. Norris Hooper, who lived at Cornbury Farm with his wife Betty, was the ARP warden. His detachment, equipped with a tin helmet and one pair of Wellington boots, was based at Lavington. Norris normally wore the tin hat, as his duties included stopping traffic at Gore Cross, and it was regarded as a sign of his authority.

By this time, Ken Mitchell was working for Major Whistler as he continued his efforts to farm beef cattle on the downs. The increase in military manoeuvres soon resulted in many badly damaged fences. Whistler therefore decided to employ two lads to watch over his herd to ensure their safety and make certain that they did not stray into dangerous training areas. Ken and his friend Jack Potter were given this job. "Sometimes we worked alone," Ken relates. "It depended on circumstances, but there was so much happening both on land and in the air that one seldom felt lonely. The main thing was to keep your eyes on the animals in your care. Once the herd had scattered it was virtually impossible for one person 'on foot' to round them up. It was a big responsibility for lads of 15: the herd amounted to around 100 animals, and at times it could have been more."

On one occasion, while watching over the herd alone, Ken had a frightening experience. It was a rainy summer evening, when the cloud was low over the Plain. He was rounding up the cattle in order to put them in a safe compound for the night when he heard the sound of aircraft engines overhead. Suddenly, an aircraft emerged out of the clouds and straight away he could see it was German by its markings. "It disappeared back into cloud," he recalls, "and I could hear it circling around as though it could be coming back again. There was an old barn almost a quarter of a mile away: it's surprising how fast you can run when you are really scared."

By the time Ken had reached the barn the aircraft had emerged from the clouds once more. "I was terrified," he states, "and remained in the barn until it was almost dark." Ken feared that if he went back into the open, one of the aircraft's gunners might take a pot shot at him. "It sounds daft!" he admits, "but I could not help thinking that the plane was looking for me."

When he did finally venture from the barn, he discovered that the herd had scattered. There was absolutely no chance of rounding them up on his own before nightfall. "As I stood there in despair," he continues, "a man appeared on a horse. It was the farm manager. He had heard the plane as well and came out to see if I was alright. With his help we soon had the herd rounded up again, and securely fenced in for the night."

On contemplation, Ken thought that the German pilot was probably looking for a local airfield to bomb at a place called New Zealand Farm, which was about two miles away. He reiterates the point that several bombs were dropped in the vicinity of the village, because it was so close to this and other military camps and facilities. "One night," he notes, "we were awakened by a strange sound that we had not heard before. It turned out to be the sound of incendiary bombs igniting. They were scattered all around the village and fortunately no serious fires were started."

A few weeks later, when workers were taking sheaves of corn from a thatched barn for threshing, they discovered one of the incendiary bombs lying among them. The bomb had penetrated the roof of the barn but failed to detonate. If a fire had started that night in a barn full of straw the consequences to the village could have been devastating, as it would almost certainly have attracted the attention of further enemy bombs.

Exactly when the idea of evacuating Imber completely was first considered can only be surmised, but the events of 13 April 1942 must surely have made it more urgent. During a demonstration on Imber Ranges, in which the RAF were to demonstrate the devastating effect that fighter aircraft equipped with cannons and machine guns could have on enemy convoys, 25 military personnel were killed. One of the inexperienced Hurricane pilots of 175 Squadron mistook a gathered crowd of military observers to be a dummy column of soldiers, and fired directly into the crowd. The demonstration was a dress rehearsal for a visit by Winston Churchill and General Marshall, Chief of Staff of the United States Army, which went ahead as planned three days later.

In September 1943, the American Army arrived on Salisbury Plain, with the 3rd Armored Division based around Warminster and the 4th Armored Division around Devizes. Imber Ranges featured extensively in their training schedules and the 1,000 yard safety net that had been placed around the village could no longer be guaranteed. It was considered too dangerous for the residents to remain, not just in the village itself, but also on the farms along what was known as the Imber Corridor.

On 1 November, the Army called a meeting at the schoolroom, announcing that the Americans needed the village to train for street fighting in Normandy, and that the 135 residents would all have to leave by 17 December. The announcement took everyone by surprise: after all, they had survived Army occupation during the First World War so why should this be any different?

Doreen Charles (nee Mitchell), who was only nine or ten at the time, notes how everyone was devastated. They had just six weeks to leave and find new homes and employment. "Thankfully everyone managed to do that," wrote Doreen. "We were promised we could return after the war but they never kept their promise. By breaking that promise in not letting us return they broke a lot of hearts, especially my dear mum. She cried for days and days after leaving. She is now lying in the cemetery at her beloved Imber. It was her home, as she was born there."

A further meeting was held at Devizes Town Hall three days later, at which a fuller explanation was offered as to why the evacuation was deemed necessary. The Army promised to assist any who were unable to find alternative accommodation, but as Doreen Charles points out, most people were able to sort something out for themselves.

The evacuation was indiscriminate and everyone had to leave, from the Deans and Hoopers, down to the poorest farm labourer. Everybody was heart broken and it is easy to understand why. Many, similar to Enos Matthews who had been employed by Sydney Dean all his working life, had never slept a night away from his cottage before.

Ken and Doreen's grandfather, Albert Nash, took it particularly badly. On the day after the meeting in Devizes, his wife Martha could not find him anywhere. She eventually went to the forge and discovered him slumped over the anvil, crying like a child. He became ill from that day and died a few weeks after the evacuation. "The doctor said of a broken heart," recalled Doreen. "He was taken back to his beloved Imber to lay to rest." Albie was the first Imber exile to return for burial in the St Giles churchyard.

Farmers were forced into selling off their stock and machinery, but as the traditional downland sheep fairs had already been held earlier in the year, everything was sold off for well below its value.

Captain Arthur Williams and his wife Hilda left Brown's Farm for a new farmhouse at Gore Cross. Sydney and Gladys Dean left Seagrams Farm and moved to Netheravon, where Sydney continued farming until his death in 1964. And Major Whistler, who had been running the Imber Court estate, moved to Everleigh.

The post office, pub, and school all sadly closed, as centuries of village life drew to an end. The Baptist chapel held its final service on 5 December 1943 at 2.30PM, while the parish church of St Giles went out with a flourish, as on 27 November it witnessed the marriage of Bernard Wright to Phyllis Daniels. Bernie had worked for Major Whistler at Imber Court Farm, and after his marriage and move to West Lavington, he secured employment with Sir Henry Holloway as a mechanic. Sir Henry was, of course, the owner of the Court before selling up to the War Office.

In May 1945, the war in Europe came to and end. By now, the majority of American soldiers in Britain had already left for the continental battlefields, and those that were still here were soon repatriated back to the United States. The Yanks were going home, but what about the people of Imber? They would soon be informed that the Army intended to retain the whole area as a permanent firing range. Therefore, re-occupation of the village by its former inhabitants was out of the question. So what about the promise the Army had made to them that they could return: indeed, was there ever a promise? In his book, *Little Imber on the Down,* Rex Sawyer gives the following explanation:

> *Perhaps there was no legally binding promise from the War Department, although tales of a letter indicating such a declaration continued to abound. Apparently, the story goes, a letter had been posted to all Imber residents before the evacuation only to be retrieved, hastily, by a red-faced military official. Such an exercise, under cover of wartime security, could have been carried out to rectify a potentially embarrassing situation at a later stage. Nevertheless there were very firm convictions among Imber folk that verbal assurances were given although difficult to confirm over 50 years later and with few villagers still alive today. The truth may well be that in getting the residents' cooperation for such an unpleasant change in their circumstances, some of the WD personnel involved at the time made statements that were reassuring and over-optimistic – if not deliberately misleading. The villagers, understandably were only too happy to adjust mentally to those most acceptable to them.*

John Williams, son of the new schoolmistress furthers:

> *On 1 November at 10.10AM she had to dismiss the children as the school was required for 'a meeting of military importance'. The promise was made that the villagers would be returning within six months or at the end of the War, depending on which came first. Well, I remember my mother holding a short Remembrance Service on 11 November and saying before we stood to observe the two minutes silence, words to the effect: 'Wouldn't it be lovely if this war was to end today so that no one would have to leave the village'. Then we sang, with her at the harmonium, 'Oh, God our help in ages past, our hope for years to come'. Every time I now hear that hymn I'm back in that little schoolroom! The halcyon days were about to be destroyed forever. I have no recollection of leaving Imber. Maybe I never did. It was obvious that the sudden and unexpected change that was taking place took its toll on my mother as it had on*

This photograph, taken outside St Giles Church in the early 1950s, consists mainly of ex-Imber residents and their relatives. The elderly lady in the front row to the right of the lady in the black coat is Ken Mitchell's grandmother, Martha Nash, and next to her is his mother Gladys Mitchell. Between them in the next row is his sister, Doreen Charles (nee Mitchell)

Photograph courtesy of Ken Mitchell

most of the Imberians. They were made to leave a way of life that had changed little for generations. The pieces of paper that the Army had circulated were quickly retrieved, someone had spoken out of turn and there was egg on the officers' faces! However, it had been said and by now it is accepted that the promise was being reneged on.

John Williams still has the entries his mother made in Imber's final school book, as well as copies of letters that she had sent to the War Department at the time. One of these letters, which was offically stamped by the WD Estate Office on 24 November 1943, includes the following:

I have received from Mr Dean, the school correspondent, three month's notice to terminate my appointment here at the school. This is dated on 20 November 1943. If after that notice expires viz 20 February 1944 I fail to obtain an alternative position are you prepared to pay my salary as I am wholly dependent of my own earnings. On the other hand if I obtain a post as assistant teacher are you prepared to make up the loss of salary as Head Teacher. Mr Dean informs me that I will get the first offer of coming back to this position after the war.

The last sentence in her letter leaves us with no doubt that Mrs Williams was under the impression that Imber would be returned to its people after the war, and the school reopened.

Initially, people seemed able to return to Imber to visit the village when the Army was not on exercise. The media of the day did not take long to show an interest in the plight of the village. In 1947, the *Wiltshire Archaeological and Natural History Magazine* noted that the place had been wantonly wrecked by vandals, "whose identity is either unknown or unrevealed."

People returning immediately after the war maintained that the Americans had treated the village with respect. So inevitably the British Army was accused of being the culprit. It was believed that many houses had been used as targets for bombers and heavy guns. The often atrocious weather on Salisbury Plain no doubt played its own part in the decline of some properties that had been left open to the elements, when doors, windows, even entire roofs had broken or collapsed. Then there was civilian vandalism. With building materials desperately short after the war, 'spivs' (for want of any better description) would wait for a lull in military training before driving their lorries along ancient trackways ignoring the 'out-of-bounds' notices, in order to rob the cottages of fittings, such as baths and fireplaces. They would also strip lead from the roofs. So in no time at all, Imber was reduced to a shadow of its former self.

At least the parish church had been boarded up and the graveyard surrounded by barbed wire. This did not prevent at least one misdirected shell from hitting it, and no doubt thieves would have gained unlawful entrance if they were determined enough. Sensibly, most material possessions had already been removed. Important documents like the parish registers and churchwarden's accounts book, which were secured in a wooden chest, were taken to Potterne Church for safekeeping. In 1952, the Rous tombs were housed in Edington church; some elaborate woodwork went to a military chapel at Bratton; and the pulpit was placed temporarily in the Army chapel at Warminster.

Imber became headline news, and Lord Long of Wraxhall raised questions in Parliament concerning the displaced residents. Eventually, tired of the bad publicity, the War Office refused any further access to the village. From that time forth, Imber was closed to everyone except ex-residents wishing to bury family members in the churchyard. Even this could only be done with written permission from the War Office, and a military escort.

In 1955, a group of villagers were given permission to return. They were able to visit the graves of their loved ones, remove the weeds and arrange flowers. The party included Martha Nash. A service was held in the church conducted by the Reverend Ralph Dudley, vicar of the newly combined parish of Edington and Imber, who reassured the congregation that treasures removed from St Giles were now safe at Edington. By 1960, these services held on the Saturday nearest to St Giles's Day became an annual pilgrimage.

Today, little of the original village remains, and its former residents would find it difficult to recognise the place. The Army continued to use the village to train in street fighting, and even built their own blocks of imitation houses, which proved very suitable to prepare soldiers for the urban warfare they faced in Northern Ireland during the 1970s and 1980s – and no doubt in Iraq at the start of the twenty-first century.

Over the years a number of people have fought very hard to get the village returned to its former inhabitants: paramount among these was councillor Austin Underwood, who organised a series of protest rallies in the 1960s. However, ultimately his efforts and those of many other individuals, were to no avail. The only way an ex-resident can be returned to Imber is to be laid to rest there. Ken and Doreen's grandfather, Albert, returned only five or six weeks after he left; their grandmother was taken back in 1967; their mother in 1982; and finally their father Fred Mitchell went home in 1983.

Although St Giles Church was made redundant in 2002, the listed 1 building is now vested into the guardianship of the Churches Conservation Trust and is undergoing a three year restoration programme which was due for completion by Easter 2008.

12

THE LOST VALLEY

Shortly after the forced evacuation of Imber, a similar fate befell the people of the Tyneham Valley in the part of south Dorset known as the Isle of Purbeck. By 1943, much of the surrounding countryside had become a well-established training area for the British Army. In particular, Bovington Camp which was inland to the north, and Bindon Range to the west.

During the First World War, due to the development of the tank and the need for an area to train tank battalions before they departed for France, the War Office began looking for a suitable site of what was considered to be unproductive land. They found the perfect location in Dorset, near the small town of Wool, the very name of which gives us a good idea of the area's prevalent industry. Expanses of open heath, interspersed with thick woodland, proved ideal. And the local villages had the same narrow streets as those that would be encountered on the continent. Undoubtedly some people – possibly shepherds – were displaced at this time but it did not affect any significant community. In due course, as the Army became permanently established in the area, a small town grew up to serve the soldiers and their families, and today the Army's re-pair workshops at Bovington Camp are among the county's largest employers.

As well as learning to drive and manoeuvre their new tanks, the crews required practice in firing their guns. For this purpose, in 1916, another area of land was requisitioned on the coast, just to the east of the famous beauty spot at Lulworth Cove. Towering above the cove to the east was a large hill capped by an Iron Age hill fort, called Bindon Hill. Here the Army established its gunnery school, which became known as Bindon Range. Tank crews were able to

Post Office Row at Tyneham and the Parish Church of St Mary in their heyday. Note the telephone box at the entrance to the post office

Photograph courtesy of Major M.H. Burgess, Range Officer, AFV Gunnery School, Lulworth Camp

shoot at targets positioned on the coastal cliffs and any shells that went 'over' dropped harmlessly into the sea beyond.

About two miles east of Bindon Range was the quiet, rural village of Tyneham, set in a beautiful and timeless valley, deep in the Purbeck Hills. Tyneham was another perfect English village, with farms, cottages, schoolhouse, post office, church and Elizabethan country manor. Here, ancient farmland met the sea, which meant that Tyneham had the best of both worlds, and although the village itself was not particularly large, the valley also included the hamlets of North and South Egliston, Povington, the fishing community of Worbarrow and several individual farms, houses and cottages dotted around the area. In 1943, one source records some 102 properties in the parish, inhabited by 252 people. As the war progressed, they must have become increasingly aware of the sound of shellfire resounding through the nearby hills, but ignorant to the fact that the Army would soon be marching east into their valley in order to expand their training facilities.

Mentioned in the Domesday Book as Tigeham, at which time it was held by Robert of Mortain, William the Conqueror's half-brother, there is a considerable amount of evidence of ancient activity throughout the area in question. For instance, there are 24 Bronze Age barrows recorded on Povington Heath, in one of which was discovered an urn now on display in the Dorset County Museum. This particular example, which is known as Povington Barrow, was around seven feet high and had a diameter of 56 feet. And just to the west of the village is Flower's Barrow, an impressive Iron Age hill fort that appears to have been dissected by coastal erosion. Therefore, we can only imagine at its original grandeur, and the former line of the cliffs. Today it looks over one of the prettiest views along the Dorset coast, with the unusual Worbarrow Tout protruding into a secluded bay, where the waters calmly trickle against the Jurassic beach. Indentations on the Tout itself are reputed to be dinosaur footprints, while towards Lulworth Cove at the foot of Bindon Hill are the remaining fragments of a fossil forest.

Other archaeological discoveries in the Tyneham Valley have included a Bronze Age pin, found in one of two large mounds on Worbarrow Cliff; seven human remains found in a mound near Tyneham church; and a small cup and a detached skull buried separately. At Worbarrow Bay, in the remains of the occupation debris of both Iron Age and Roman settlement, finds have included pottery, sling stones, spindle whorls, a fragment of an armlet, an iron knife, a stone handmill, a loom weight, and a coin of Commodus. Flanged bowls dating from the third or fourth centuries have been found, and most unusually an urn filled with what were initially thought to be black coins, but later identified as the fragments that remained after cutting rings for personal ornaments.

An abundance of Celtic field systems, principally at Gold Down, mostly later overlain with strip lynchets, show that the valley has been farmed since at least the fifth century BC. This would have been a mixture of arable farming, mostly growing corn, with flocks of sheep grazing the surrounding hills. But no doubt cattle and pigs were also farmed. Little therefore had changed by 1900.

As with many traditional English country villages, the big house or manor was very much at Tyneham's centre. The last owner of Tyneham House was W.R.G. Bond, who was evacuated from his home, along with the rest of the village just before Christmas 1943. Before the Norman conquest, after which the land had passed to Robert Mortain, it had belonged to a Saxon noble called Alnod. By the middle of the fourteenth century, a wooden hall was known to have existed, built by the Russell family, but the Tudor manor was built between 1567 and 1583 by Henry Williams. So it had passed through several hands until 1683, when it came into the possession of Nathaniel Bond of Lutton. The Bond's therefore remained in ownership right up until 1952, when it was compulsory purchased by the War Office.

During the war, W.R.G. Bond's son Mark, who had hoped to someday inherit his father's estate, was serving in the Army himself, having joined the Rifle Brigade on leaving Eton in 1940. He and his father had taken up residence in 1937, following the death of his grandfather in 1935. The reason for this two-year gap was that, in order to pay death duties, they had to raise the necessary funds by renting the house out. Ironically, in the same post that brought a letter informing Mr Bond that he would have to leave his house within 28 days, he also received a telegram reporting that his son was "missing in action." Mark Bond, who remained in the Army after the war, attaining the rank of major general, spent the rest of the hostilities in a German prisoner of war camp.

The parish church of St Mary the Virgin provided the focus of community life in the village for hundreds of years. It also attracted attendees from outlying communities, such as Povington, Worbarrow and South Egliston. Originally, the parish had belonged to the Diocese of Bristol, before transferring to the Diocese of Salisbury in 1836. As the most influential family in the parish, the pews in the north transept were reserved for the Bonds. However, in the late eighteenth century, which coincided with the rectorship of William Bond, it was decided that the seating in the church was inadequate. To compensate for this, a south transept was built and the Bond family pews were moved there accordingly. After that, the pews in the north transept were always referred to as the 'cowstalls', which were thereafter occupied by all other parishioners, including the family of the presiding rector. It is quite possible that the church began life as a private chapel belonging to the manor house. Its first rector, William de Cane, was appointed in 1304 and the last, Humphrey Churchill Money, in 1937.

Understandably, there are several splendid monuments dedicated to members of the Bond family both inside and outside the church. The sanctuary, for instance, contains a lancet window in remembrance of Nathaniel Bond. The chancel once boasted a fine pipe organ that was donated in thanks for the safe homecoming of Captain Algernon Bond who, although severely wounded, survived the Siege of Ladysmith during the South African War. This organ has now been installed at nearby Steeple church. Other monuments reflect those who served the family, such as Elizabeth Tarrant, whose 34 years of faithful service to Mrs Bond was recorded on a stone tablet in the nave; and Hannah Hunworth, nurse to the Bond family for many years, commemorated by a further tablet.

In 1910, a coronation tree was planted near the church to commemorate the coronation of King George v; and at the invitation of the Army, Major General Bond planted a Silver Jubilee Oak near the current visitor car park in 1977. Also near the church, set in a niche in a stone wall, was the village tap from which water could be drawn. This tap was supplied by a small reservoir cut into the hillside, and an inscription above it reads: "Whosoever drinketh of this water shall thirst again, but whosoever drinketh of the water that I shall give him shall never thirst."

Similar to other small rural villages, many jobs were provided up at the big house or on the local farm, who were often the same employer. The biggest farm employer in the valley was Tyneham Farm, which although owned by the Bond family was managed by Walter Smith, who was regarded by his workers as strict but fair. It was a large farm of some 3,000 acres and had several closed-in yards. There was a stable yard, a rickyard and a cow yard. The great barn had a granary above it, which was reached from a stone staircase ascending the outside wall.

It was a mixed farm, with corn being the predominant crop. Harvesting and haymaking towards the end of summer would have been the busiest time of the year, and farmer Smith was known to allow his workers to drink cider while working in the fields during the long hours this entailed. Soon afterwards, the whole valley would reverberate to the sound of a steam-operated threshing machine. In the early part of the twentieth century, teams of heavy horses did most of the work, but unusually for such a remote village, Tyneham did not have its own blacksmith. If a horse required shoeing, the farrier would come from the village of East Creech.

Milk from the dairy herd would be delivered to the village of Corfe Castle in horse drawn milk carts, where it was loaded onto a steam train bound for London. Later, a dairy was opened in Corfe Castle itself. Once a week, calves suckled up from the dairy cows were driven to Wool station and from there transported to Dorchester market. Also bound for the county town would be pigs, lambs and fleeces, all depending on the time of year. Farm labourers had few days off, but one annual highlight was Woodbury Fair at Bere Regis in September.

Before a village hall was built in 1926, the barn at Tyneham Farm was often used to perform plays and pantomimes. Indeed, some of these were put on in order to raise money for the building of the hall. And at Christmas, a traditional mummers' play would also be staged here as well. The mummers would recite ancient words passed down through the generations, now largely forgotten.

At the end of the nineteenth century, a Miss Mary Cooper was employed at Tyneham House as a housemaid. At that time the Coopers were a large family in the area. Mary was married at Hurst Tarrant, Hampshire, in 1897. She met her husband after he came to the village to work as a groom. Their grandson, William Hayter, explains that both of his great great grandparents are buried in Tyneham churchyard. There are further Coopers buried both there and in the next village of Steeple. "The last gravestone of a Cooper I could find in Tyneham," he explains, "was a young lady in 1928." A few years ago, while visiting the village, Mr Hayter found that some flowers had been placed on the grave, so it appears that other descendants of the Cooper family also show an interest: but he does not know who they are.

The telephone box at Tyneham today, dutifully preserved as it appeared in the 1940s, before the eviction

The wedding of Tyneham girl, Mary Cooper, at Hurst Tarrant, Hampshire in 1897. Mary Cooper was a house maid at Tyneham House and met her husband when he came to the village to work as a groom

Photograph courtesy of William Hayter

Tyneham was made up of several groups of cottages, but the main street just below the church consisted of four cottages, called Post Office Row. Built in local rough stone, they would originally have been thatched, with their roofs later replaced with slates.

The first of these cottages was traditionally the home of the shepherd. He also had a sheephouse in the hills, surrounded by lambing pens, where he would spend long days and nights during the lambing season. The Tyneham flock is said to have numbered 700 animals. Shepherd Lucas was a revered authority and lived in the cottage for many years; his wife acted as a voluntary district nurse, to whom people would come with minor ailments.

The next cottage was the tiny post office and village shop. From here, Mrs Driscoll, the last postmistress, would supply the village with many of their day to day requirements. The post office also had a telephone in the kitchen, which was only used for sending and receiving telegrams. In the 1940s, a new public telephone box was installed in front of the post office. This odd looking construction, still preserved in its original state, looks as though it belonged to an earlier decade – the 1920s or 1930s – rather than the 1940s, by which time traditional red boxes were already in common use around the country. You could buy most daily essentials in the shop, while some by-products of local agriculture, such as milk, cheese and eggs, were all available from the dairy at Tyneham Farm, as were salted fish.

The Hollands lived in the third cottage, which was reserved for a farm worker and his family. Percy Holland had been employed at Tyneham Farm since he was 11, working his way up to become the carter in charge of all the working horses on the estate, which at the time was a serious responsibility. His mother, known as 'Granny Holland', was the local midwife and would deliver the babies of the parish in the absence of the doctor.

And the final house in the row was reserved for the schoolteacher, with its garden conveniently backing on to the village school, which is today preserved by the Army as a museum. The school itself closed in 1932, its final schoolmistress being Miss Hearne. By this time there were not enough children to make it viable.

The school was built in 1860 by the rector of the time, the Reverend Nathaniel Bond, on glebeland close to the church, using materials reclaimed from an old tithe barn. Bond paid for the building of the school himself, and although the teacher, James Roe, ran it with the help of one lady assistant, Nathaniel Bond was himself very involved with the welfare of the village children. The building consisted of one large room, in which today examples of the work done by the children are on display, along with posters and other contemporary teaching aids. At one end of the room was a raised platform on which the infants would sit. This would also be used as a stage to put on school productions, and in the evenings the schoolroom was sometimes opened up as a reading room, or in the winter somewhere for the young men of the village to gather to play table games. At the other end of the school is a narrow cloakroom where the names of all the children are displayed against their coat pegs.

In the winter, the valley could be quite a wild place, so attendance for some children coming in from outlying hamlets and farms could be unpredictable. Also, during harvesting and haymaking many children would be out in the fields helping their parents; and when the threshing machine arrived, the excitement would have been too great for many children to contain. But there were many other reasons that might also have affected attendance – for instance, one entry in the school book dated 26 September 1913 noted that Ernest Jewer had not attended school since the end of the summer holiday because he had no boots. By contrast, also displayed in the school is the exemplary attendance certificate of Frederick Knight, who was the son of the Bond's coachman. He lived at Museum Cottage, which was between Tyneham House and Farm, so presumably absenteeism for him was not an option for anything other than genuine sickness.

Among the pieces of work on display at the school written by the pupils, all of which relate to the area's wildlife, is one by Jim Wellman. The Isle of Purbeck is still famous for its diversity of creatures and their habitats, and Jim, whose age we do not know, wrote about the badgers. His spelling left a lot to be desired, and the bracketed words are just a few of the suggested alterations written on the essay in red ink, presumably my Miss Hearne:

I called for Arthur next door and us (we) went to look for badgers dung pit. Mam says as us (that we) shouldn't play there because its where them (they) does their toilet. My dad had a hege (hedge) up Baltington Farm over one of they (their) paths. Badgers kept coming back at night and bashing down my dad's hege cos (because) it was on one of badgers paths and my dad says as how they alus (always) goes walking on the same paths and wont go different for anything. I have done a drawing of a fern growing by badgers sett. It is called Harts Tongue.

The Wellmans lived at the Gwyle Cottages mentioned later, where their neighbours were the Goulds. Baltington Farm was another property to the west of Tyneham, which in earlier times may well have been a larger settlement in its own right. At the bottom of Jim's essay, the teacher had commented: "Well done, write your spellings three times each." But at least he was right about the badgers usually treading their own well-trampled paths.

Other properties in the village included the rectory, which might have appeared somewhat grand for such a small village, although the vicar also covered services at Steeple and Grange from 1738 onwards. This new rectory, which reflected the social status often awarded to Victorian country pastors, had its own tennis court and formal gardens, tended by John Gould. It was built around 1880 and before that the rector and his family lived in another building, which thereafter became a row of cottages known as Rectory Cottages. However, the rector's social status certainly was not reflected in his salary, so in order to supplement his income he would rent out the new rectory to wealthy visitors during the summer months, while he and his family would relegate themselves to life at the cottages. Having said that, three members of the Bond family were rectors at various times, and would undoubtedly have been men of private means. Nathaniel Bond, rector from 1852–89, was certainly known to be a benefactor to the village.

Most village houses had a link to either Tyneham House or Farm, such as the oddly named Laundry Cottages. From here, two sisters – Elizabeth and Helen Taylor – did the laundry for the big house. The laundry was delivered to them every Monday morning by their stepbrother, Charlie Meech. Charlie was employed by the Bonds as a general handyman, and he would transport the weekly laundry by horse and cart. The Taylor sisters had inherited these duties from their mother after she died in 1917. Their father had been the estate woodman.

Then there was Gardener's Cottage, the residence of Tom Gould, the head gardener at Tyneham House, which having extensive lawns as well as a shrubbery, vegetable gardens and orchards containing a variety of fruit trees. And at Double Cottages, the widow Davis brought up her five children. Every day in the early morning and afternoon, she worked at Tyneham Farm as a milkmaid. Her son, Jack Davis, who also worked on the farm, was recorded as driving the first tractor in the valley.

As you entered the village from the southern end there was a substantial village pond, where during the evenings Percy Holland and others would bring the working horses for a well-deserved drink after they finished in the fields. The villagers, including Henry Miller, a fisherman from Worbarrow, would sink hazel faggots in this pond, which would be hoisted out a few days later, hopefully revealing any eels that were caught between them. The pond was well-known for its eels and the fishermen would use them for baiting their crab or lobster pots.

A stream trickled out of the pond towards the sea, its course following a gully known as Tyneham Gwyle. Along its course are two further cottages, known as the Gwyle Cottages, in one of which lived the Goulds – a family of successful gardeners. Tom, of course, became the head gardener at Tyneham House, at which time he went to live at Gardener's Cottage, while his son John worked for the rector. In the cottage next door lived the Wellman family. Mrs Wellman, the daughter of Shepherd Lucas, worked in service at the big house; followed there by her daughter Rose after she left school at 14. And from Jim Wellman's school essay it is likely that his father worked at Baltington or another of the valley's farms.

Further along the Gwlye towards the fishing hamlet of Worbarrow were Gate Cottage and Fern Hollow. Gate Cottage, which had its own deep well, was the home of the Warr family; the father being another handyman on the estate. And Charlie and Harriet Miller lived at Fern Hollow. The Millers were the predominant fishing family at the hamlet, but as well as fishing, Charlie and his wife apparently earned a little extra money by selling postcards, sweets and chocolates to the visitors who came to admire the beauty of Worbarrow Bay. Fossil hunters, nature lovers, and people simply interested in taking the sea air would have been a common fixture.

One wealthy lady, Mrs Wheeler, took up permanent residence in a large building on the cliff, deceptively named The Bunaglow. The villagers held Mrs Wheeler in high regard, in spite of the differences between them socially and financially. She was known to have held Christmas parties for their children and sent people soup when they were ill. She also provided the wedding cake when her parlour-maid, Flo Davis, was married.

Warwick Draper built Sheepleaze in 1910. His granddaughter, Meg Kingston, remembers visiting the house as a young girl during holidays. Her mother was Mary Draper and her uncle Philip Draper, the eldest of the children. Once Meg discovered a small cave in the boulders between Worbarrow Bay and Hobarrow Bay, which being such a tiny gap, she failed to find a second time. But she remembers that inside the cave was a rough wooden bench, and her mother told her that brandy would have been hidden here in the days of smuggling. "My mother," she explains, "told me that smuggling still went on when she was a child. The coastguards, so she said, would turn a blind eye to various goings on and in the morning a keg of brandy would be deposited on their doorsteps."

In the church is a beautiful east window, which was donated in memory of Mrs Draper of Worbarrow. It depicts the Madonna and Child, on either side of which are panels designed by Christopher Draper, illustrating scenes from Tyneham life, showing a farm labourer and a fisherman busy at work.

The main hamlet of Worbarrow was situated right on the bay, just before reaching the Tout, which was a limestone hill protruding into the sea, joined to the mainland by a thin neck of land. From here a small group of fishermen caught crabs, lobsters and mackerel. The seaward side of the hamlet was fronted by a row of fine cottages that were used as a coastguard station until 1911 and occupied by retired Royal Navy seamen and their families. In front of these cottages was a small boathouse and a stone slipway. A handrail aided the climb up some steps to the top of the Tout where the coastguard posted a lookout and had a flagstaff and signal canon. With an uninterrupted view along the coast, it was also a good place to keep an eye open for shoals of mackerel as they came close to shore. Henry Miller, the oldest member of Worbarrows' fishing dynasty, often performed this task, calling the boats into action as soon as he spotted the tell-tale signs.

Henry lived with his wife Louisa in a cottage at the foot of Gold Down. He had two sons, Tom, who at the time of the evacuation was still living with his parents; and Jack, who lived with his wife Alice at Sea Cottage – aptly the nearest dwelling to the water's edge. Alice Rose was nicknamed Miggie, and when she and Jack married they had originally moved into Rose Cottage with Miggie's mother, Granny Rose. However, following the death of Jack's cousin Joe, resulting from a poisoned finger, they at last had a place of their own. Jack and Miggie were well loved throughout the community and visitors to their woodshed were invited to a glass of home-brewed beer. No doubt Granny Rose was an occasional visitor as she is reputed to have enjoyed a tipple. Summer visitors often lodged at Sea Cottage with Jack and Miggie, who could cook a four-course meal on their little cottage stove. In her younger days, Alice had worked as a cook at a hotel in Swanage. In fact, it was there that she met her future husband, who at the time was working for the same hotel as a coachman.

From her childhood holidays at Sheepleaze, Meg Kingston has particular memories of visiting Miggie and Jack, who was known to her as Jam. "I do remember their small cosy kitchen," she states, "with the smell of oil, coal and the sea. I would be given a Dads Cookie biscuit from a tin above the solid fuel cooker, while various cats wandered in and out. I visited Jack and Miggie after they were re-housed inland from Swanage. Jack led up to a top window in the attic from which he could just see the sea – sad for one who had always lived so closely with it."

The Mintern family lived in another cottage at Worbarrow and grazed a small herd of cows at various locations around the hamlet and at Tyneham itself. They would provide milk to the villagers, which their lodger Arthur Stockley would take around to each cottage in buckets, using a pint ladle to measure it into the jugs of their customers.

For most people in the valley, even during the 1940s, life was often a struggle. Conditions were primitive, amenities and services few and far between, material possessions rare, and wages were little more than sufficient to cover the barest of essentials. Yet, the village had a great spirit and sense of community, which helped them to cope with the privations of rural life. So in 1943, all of the families at Tyneham and Worbarrow, from the Bonds to the Millers, as well as others living at Povington, Lutton, North and South Egliston, and other isolated properties in the valley, found themselves in the spotlight as the War Office decided to extend its firing capacity to the east, thus creating a larger training area today known as the Lulworth Ranges. Unlike Imber, where most people had a shrewd idea of what could happen to their village because of its vicinity to the Army's training facilities on Salisbury Plain, the ordinary working families at Tyneham were taken by almost complete surprise. At Imber, convoys of vehicles passed daily through the main street and the War Office had already purchased all the properties. Tyneham, on the other hand, was

Sheep grazing at Flower's Barrow, above Worbarrow Bay. The fishing hamlet of Worbarrow stood near the neck of land attached to Worbarrow Tout. The remains of one or two buildings can still be found there

Photograph courtesy of Jim Champion

quiet and relatively untouched by the presence of the Army. The villagers were, of course, well aware that a tank firing range existed over the western horizon, but they themselves rarely came into contact with anyone from the military.

In mid-November 1943, all residents of the Tyneham valley received an unexpected letter from Major-General C.H. Miller, from the Army's Southern Command, which, after explaining the reasons why they needed to expand their training facilities – and explaining how they had carefully searched to find an area that would effect the least amount of people – included the following statement:

> *It is regretted that, in the National Interest, it is necessary to move you from your homes, and everything possible will be done to help you, both by payment of compensation, and by finding other accommodation for you if you are unable to do so yourself. The date on which the military will take over this area is the 19th December next, and all civilians must be out of the area by that date. A special office will be opened at Westportt House, Wareham, on Wednesday 17th November, and you will be able to get advice between the hours of 10AM and 7PM, from there on your personal problems and difficulties. Any letters should be sent to that address also for the present.*
>
> *The Government appreciate that this is no small sacrifice which you are asked to make, but they are sure that you will give this further help towards winning the war with a good heart.*

There is no mention in the letter as to whether or not the people of Tyneham would be permitted back to their homes after the war. Yet similar to Imber, this seems to have been the assumption. It has to be remembered also that the Army's expansion at the time not only affected the valley itself, but an area north of Whiteway, which nestled at the head of the valley. Over the hills at this point, the training area took in a large area of open heathland, which became known as Heath Range. In total, the Lulworth Ranges now covered 7,500 acres of land, including a shore line stretching some six and a half miles between Lulworth Cove and Kimmeridge Bay.

All of the residents complied with War Office demands, some being rehoused in new council houses built in Sandford near Wareham, others going to Swanage, Kimmeridge, and other destinations further afield. When they finally vacated the village just before Christmas 1943, they famously pinned the following notice to the door of St Mary's Church, written by Evelyn Bond: "Please treat the church and houses with care; we have given up our homes where many of us lived for generations to help win the war to keep men free. We shall return one day and thank you for treating the village kindly."

Any hope that the villagers had of ever returning home was dashed in 1948 when the entire valley received a compulsory purchase order from the Army. However, the former residents did not concede without a fight, and during the intervening years several campaigns have been launched on their behalf. A Tyneham Action Group was formed in May 1968, and in 1970, the prime minister Edward Heath, himself an ex-soldier, set up the Nugent Defence Lands Committee, which set about investigating whether or not any holdings belonging to the Ministry of Defence could be returned to private ownership.

In July 1973, the valley came closest to being released, as the Nugent Committee concluded that the Lulworth Ranges could indeed be closed. They proposed moving the gunnery school to Castlemartin in Dyfed. The Welsh authorities were opposed to this move, and Dorset County Council strongly felt that the area would suffer economically if the Army left. So in 1974, the government published a white paper which said that it was unable to accept the recommendation that the gunnery school should be moved from Lulworth to Castlemartin. Instead, they agreed that the Army should continue to use the Lulworth Ranges, but that the general public should have some access to the land also. To look into this a working party was set up consisting of representatives from the Countryside Commission, the Nature Conservancy Council, Dorset County Council, Purbeck District Council, Department of the Environment and the Army (resulting from this working party was the establishment of the Lulworth Range Walks).

Although the Army still uses the ranges extensively for training purposes, during most weekends and several other specified periods of the year the general public is allowed access to the village and the surrounding countryside by following specially marked paths. And, of course, it is possible to visit Worbarrow Bay and its tranquil beach. The houses now appear as a series of ghostly ruins, but both the church and school have been preserved and their exhibitions present a view of life in the Tyneham valley as it once was in the early twentieth century.

*Yr Eifl and Llanaelhaearn under snow. Nant Gwrtheyrn lies
between the mountain and the sea behind*

Photograph courtesy of Dr Carl Iwan Clowes

13

A LAND OF
DRAGONS AND KINGS

At the turn of the twentieth century, at places like Morwellham Quay and Dylife, the metallic ore deposits that had sustained the life of the villages was running out and mines were closing down. However, in some parts of Britain, mining villages continued to thrive while the natural resource they provided remained in demand. This was often the case for some quarrying and coal mining settlements. Coal mining villages remained secure because the coal itself was the driving force behind some industries or power supplies. Similarly, many areas that had grown around quarries were also expanding because of the growth of distant towns and cities, and their need for mass quantities of stone and granite, especially for road building.

In north Wales, just south of Caernarfon, the Llyn Peninsula juts into the sea between St George's Channel and the Irish Sea, and like an accusing finger points towards Ynys Enlli, the island of Bardsey. Along the peninsula's northern coast, between the sea and the slopes of a mountain called Yr Eifl, is the dramatic setting for the village of Nant Gwrtheyrn, sometimes called Porth-y-Nant. This general area is known colloquially as the 'Nant', and before the village was built it was home to a small farming community. That was until industrialists in the nineteenth century began to exploit the huge reserves of granite that formed the cliffs and mountains around. The village had two rows of houses, a larger mansion house or 'plas', a school, a chapel, a bakehouse and a cooperative shop. But even so, the last people moved from here in 1959 and for the next 20 years most of the properties, now abandoned, fell into serious disrepair. A generation of hippies moved in and established the New Atlantis Commune. Further deterioration in the fabric ensued until the late John Lennon reputedly bought an island in Clew Bay, Ireland, for the 'community'. Then in 1978, the entire village was bought by a Trust and became the home of the National Centre for Welsh Language and Culture.

To have a centre for Welsh culture in the Nant is particularly relevant, as it has an ancient and colourful history, worthy of a brief mention before exploring the latter day settlement. Much of the following is therefore derived from the research of Professor Bedwyr Lewis Jones and Elen Rhys, for Cwmni Acen of Cardiff, the On-line Language Centre for Wales who hold courses at the centre. Although Professor Jones is sadly no longer with us, the research is used by permission of Elen Rhys, in consultation with both Acen and the Professor's wife. Elen Rhys explained that "Bedwyr was a people's academic and would, I know, be delighted to see the stories and histories reaching a wider audience." I hope therefore that my very abbreviated account of the Nant will do him justice.

Long before the Nant's granite was being extracted, Yr Eifl provided local people with another valuable resource, as large quantities of iron ore had been discovered there. Evidence suggests that, as early as 150 BC, local warring kings depended on this iron both for weapons to fight their enemies and to sell. By the fourth century AD an entire network of roads had been built by the Romans around Wales in order to transport this iron. Such roads linked Caernarfon with places like Meirionnydd, Brecon and Ceredigion.

In the *Mabinogion,* which is a collection of Welsh tales dating from Celtic times translated by Lady Charlotte Guest in the mid nineteenth century from two earlier documents, *The Red Book of Hergest* and *The White Book of Rhydderch,* there is a story featuring Elen Luyddog, the daughter of King Eudaf. She fell in love with Macsen Wledig and according to the story, persuaded him to build a road to carry metal out of the district.

In 383 AD Macsen Wledig left Britain for France and took his army with him, where he eventually died. Elen and her two brothers, Cynan and Gadeon, had accompanied him. Another ancient manuscript, the *Notitia Dignitatum,* dated at around 429 AD, mentions that an army from Caernarfon had left for the continent, which presumably was King Eudaf's own army. His son, Cynan, was known to have settled in the area around Nantes in France. One story tells of how Cynan ruled that if any local girl married one of his soldiers her tongue would have to be cut out to make sure that her children would only speak their father's language!

If this was all true, it meant that while King Eudaf's army was in France, the area of north Wales which included the Nant was now largely unprotected from invaders from Ireland. To help in their fight against these invaders, Cunedda's army arrived from southern Scotland at the invitation of 'Gwrtheyrn'. Presumably, this is among the first recorded uses of the title Gwrtheyrn. Professor Jones and Elen Rhys explain that: "When the Romans departed they left Britain in the charge of local stewards who inevitably gained considerable power. It is possible that some may have had the title 'Gwrtheyrn' placed upon them – 'gor' is 'super' and 'teyrn' means 'king'. There was definitely more than one Gwrtheyrn."

According to one source Gwrtheyrn y Nant was one of these stewards, and had originally lived in Kent in the fifth century. In order to protect his land in the troubled times that followed the departure of the Romans, he decided to hire mercenaries from Germania and Saxony. In return for their help Gwrtheyrn y Nant gave these men land on the Isle of Thanet near Hastings. One of the mercenary leaders was a man called Hengist, and Gwrtheyrn y Nant fell in love with his daughter Alys Rhonwen. He asked for her hand in marriage, which was agreed and a great feast was arranged to celebrate the occasion. But Hengist and Alys planned a massacre. During the feast they arranged for every Briton to sit next to one of their own men, then at a given point each man from Germania drew concealed daggers and killed the man sat next to him. Luckily, Gwrtheyrn y Nant escaped the massacre and fled with his family and druids.

After this event history paints the picture that Britain was now open to invasion from the Saxons who came from modern day Germany, and during the following centuries the Celts were slowly driven into Wales, Cornwall and Scotland. Someone had to be blamed for this situation, and the name of Gwrtheyrn y Nant became notorious in legend as the Celtic king of Britain who betrayed his own people to the Saxons. Through history this led to the traditional idea that the Welsh were largely descended from the Celts and the English from the Saxons, and in some parts of Wales the English were often called 'the children of Alys'.

But what actually happened to Gwrtheyrn y Nant himself after escaping the massacre? On the advice of his druids he fled to the farthest point of the country to build a fort. His journey took him through Wales until he reached the mountains of Snowdonia, which he considered ideal for the construction of this fort. His followers set to work but the building was hampered by a series of mishaps, as their construction kept collapsing and disappearing mysteriously into the ground. He then encountered a young magician, a fatherless boy called Emrys Wledig, who told him that there was an underground lake beneath the fort's foundations in which dwelt two sleeping dragons. Gwrtheyrn decided to drain the lake, which effectively released the dragons who proceeded to fight each other fiercely in the sky. There was a white dragon and a red dragon, which in legend came to represent the Saxons or English, and the Welsh. The red dragon of new Wales was victorious. The powerful magician built his own fort called Dinas Emrys, which was said to be opposite Llyn Dinas near Beddgelert, and Gwrtheyrn was forced to continue his travels.

Professor Jones and Elen Rhys explain that the *Historia Brittonum* mentions "Gwrtheyrn travelling with his druids and reaching the district of 'Guunnessi'. The location of Guunnessi was not known until 1963 when Professor Melville Richards showed that the name was still alive in the name of a farm called Gwynnys near the road from Llithfaen to Nefyn."

If true, this brings Gwrtheyrn y Nant to the slopes of Yr Eifl and the area where the village of Nant Gwrtheyrn would bear his name many centuries later. Perhaps he settled here after hearing of the iron that was being dug from the hills. With this iron he would be able to equip his army and stand ready against invaders. But as with all legendary figures, his life and death are enveloped with mystery. There are two stories that tell of his final days. In one, god sent fire from heaven to burn him, signified perhaps by the lightning storms which occur in the Nant. While trying to flee from the area, Gwrtheyrn and his son were killed by Garmon, one of the local leaders. In the other version, Gwrtheyrn was tormented by a broken heart after opening the doors of Britain to the Saxons. He lost his mind and roamed the mountains, finally disappearing from the pages of history. However, in the 1770s, while travelling through north Wales writing his *Tours of Wales*, Thomas Pennant came across a cairn or tumulus near the sea at Nant Gwrtheyrn. This was a stone grave covered with earth which the locals called Gwrtheyrn's Grave. Apparently Pennant had been told that the people of the Nant had opened the grave in which they found a coffin containing the bones of a tall man. After this the spot was marked on Ordnance Survey maps as Gwrtheyrn's Castle. So, was this the final resting place of this tragic Celtic king?

After the death of Gwrtheyrn there are many stories connected with the Nant during the dark and middle ages, but we leap ahead to 1776 when Pennant wrote a description of its inhabitants in his *Tours of Wales*, at which time there appear to have been three farms. "Three families live on the land as tenants," he wrote, "growing corn and keeping a few cows, sheep and goats. They find it very difficult to get their small amount of produce to the market."

Life was a struggle and the Nant was considered isolated and difficult to reach. To survive there the people had to become self-sufficient, making their own butter and bread, and salting their meat. There was no coal in the area, so peat and cow dung was burned for heating, and bundles of straw, heather, fern and gorse were lit as torches. When the fires died out in the three farms, fire had to be carried from a cottage at the foot of Yr Eifl. According to Elen Evans who lived in the Nant at the turn of the twentieth century, this was the way of life until the quarries opened.

The romantic isolation of the Nant became the background for one of the most famous and sombre love stories in Welsh history, the story of Rhys and Meinir. The three farms on the Nant were called Ty Hen, Ty Canol and Ty Uchaf. Rhys Maredydd was an orphaned boy who lived on one of these farms. A girl called Meinir lived on one of the other farms with her father. Rhys and Meinir were the same age, but they were also cousins. When they were children they played together, gradually falling in love as they developed into teenagers. A date was set for their wedding and preparations begun. The inviter was Ifan y Cilie, and his duty was to wander around the district bearing the good news and informing every household that the couple were to be married in St Beuno's Church in Clynnog on a chosen Saturday. Professor Jones and Elen Rhys wrote:

Some of the neighbours were invited down to the 'Nant' before the wedding to give gifts to the young couple. They all came, one giving a piece of cloth, another bringing some yeast flour, everyone bringing useful things. Food was plentiful in the 'Nant' and all the guests and family were looking forward to the joyful occasion on the following day. The morning of the wedding arrived. The weather was fine as Rhys started his journey to the church in Clynnog. Meinir was in her father's house awaiting Rhys' friends to come on horseback to take her to the church. As she caught sight of the group galloping down into the 'Nant', she ran to hide as was traditionally expected of her. The group went to the house to sing penillion and Meinir's father tried his best to keep them out by answering each verse. When they eventually entered the house they found that Meinir had gone. After searching for a long time, they believed that Meinir had been cleverer than them and had gone to the church without them. However, Meinir was not in Clynnog and people began to worry. Rhys and his friends ran back to the 'Nant' and searched again, but to no avail. By the morrow, it became obvious that something had happened to Meinir. Rhys never gave up looking and as a result he lost his mind. He wandered all over the 'Nant' night and day shouting 'Meinir, Meinir'. Months went by. Rhys would often go to a hollow oak tree above the sea where he and Meinir used to meet.

One stormy night, Rhys was sitting under the hollow tree when a storm took hold and a bolt of lightning struck it and split it open. The skeleton of Meinir fell out of the tree wearing her wedding dress. It is said that this was the end for Rhys. He died there, at that moment, from a broken heart, and the lovers were buried together in the same grave. It is interesting to note that the story contains elements of other tales from the Nant, one of which involved three monks. During a journey to a monastery on Ynys Enlli, the monks wished to build a church at the Nant, but the local people threw stones at them. In return the monks cast three curses on the Nant, one of which was that members of the same family would not be allowed to marry one another.

The tale of the two tragic lovers was first published in Welsh under the title *Priodas yn Nant Gwrtheyrn,* or *A Wedding in Nant Gwrtheyrn,* in a collection of folk stories called *Cymru Fu 1862–64,* or *A Wales that Was.* The author was not known, although he was believed to have been Owen Wyn Jones of Glasynys. The same story had already appeared in English under the title *The Bride of Nant Gwrtheyrn,* and the lovers' names in this version were Rees and Margaret. This version concludes with the claim of a fisherman that he had seen a skeleton moving across the beach at Nant Gwrtheyrn when he was out on the sea. People have also allegedly seen two ghosts moving hand in hand, one of them being a man with a beard and long hair, and the other a woman with hollow sockets for her eyes. It is also believed that no birds would land on the bark of the hollow tree except the owl and the cormorant.

Above: Nant Gwrtheyrn (Porth y Nant) viewed from the top before descending the new road
Below: the former 'shippon' at Nant Gwrtheyrn in ruins – now developed as Caffi Meinir for visitors to the centre

Photographs courtesy of Dr Carl Iwan Clowes

Former resident of Nant Gwrtheyrn gazing at the village in ruins

Photograph courtesy of Dr Carl Iwan Clowes

The secluded rural life in the Nant came to an end when quarrying began in earnest. Cities like Manchester and Liverpool were developing rapidly and vast quantities of granite were required for road building. Many of the roads were built by using large rectangular blocks of granite called 'setts'. Several quarries were opened in the Nant, which as well as having a vast reserve of granite, was close to the sea making transportation easier than by road. So, as well as the quarry at Nant Gwrtheyrn which opened around 1850, there were workings at Penmaenmawr and another above Trefor.

Several attempts were made to open a setts works at Nant Gwrtheyrn. First to try was Hugh Owen from Anglesey, but others followed, until around 1861 a company called Kneeshaw and Lupton from Liverpool began developing the area. So a quarry was opened and a jetty built into the sea from where the setts could be loaded onto ships. Soon afterwards a row of houses was built on even land near the shore to house the first workers. These houses were called Holyhead View but were commonly known as the Barics. There were 13 small houses between two bigger ones, built in the shape of an I. Most of the original workers came from Ireland, although many Welshmen were also attracted because the money was better than on the farms. Some local men would arrive on Monday morning, bringing enough food to last the working week. They would remain in the Barics until Saturday before returning home to their families. At first all the inhabitants were male, but soon their wives would follow. Kneeshaw and Lupton gave their growing village the more English sounding name of Port Nant, and before long over 60 new people swelled the Nant's population from the 16 who had previously lived on the three farms.

The three quarries that opened around Nant Gwrtheyrn were called Cae'r Nant, Porth y Nant and Carreg y Llam, and large ships would carry their setts to Manchester, Liverpool, Birkenhead and beyond. The workings were so successful that, in 1878, another 24 houses were built in two rows. These were built in the shape of an L, with Sea View looking out to sea and Mountain View facing the quarry. A separate and larger house was built for the quarry manager on land at the end of Mountain View, which was called the Plas, while at the end of Sea View a larger house called Bay View had a shop and bakery behind it.

By the time of the census taken in 1886, there were 200 people living in the Nant, which included the inhabitants of the three farms and around 190 quarry workers and their families. At this point the majority of the inhabitants were Welsh speaking, largely originating from other parts of the Llyn Peninsula, such as Pistyll and Edern. But they also came from Penmaenmawr in Arfon and from farms on Anglesey. Many others had come from Scotland, Ireland or England, notably from Mount Sorrell in Leicestershire.

"Some of the workers were miners and their job was to drag down the rock," explains Professor Jones and Elen Rhys. "They did this by boring a hole through the rock with a gimlet; one would drive a sledgehammer while the other turned the gimlet. Then they would have to hang from a rope and place gunpowder and a fuse in the hole and light it. Each different 'ponc' (gallery) of the rock had its own name - Bonc Isa, Bonc Bach, Bonc Sir Fôn, Bonc Buenos Aires and so on. The rock would fall in various shapes and sizes. The next task was to break the stone lumps into shaped setts of a particular size, and this was the setter's job using various hammers. When the setts were ready they were put on wagons which ran down to the jetty on rails."

Many ships would tie up to the jetty and leave again laden with setts, but they would also bring supplies from Liverpool. Because of this people from all over the area, including farmers, would flock to the village whenever a ship came in. At such times, the number of people would have swelled considerably and the shore would have been a bustling hive of activity. One of these ships was the *Amy Summerfield.* On a particularly stormy night she came into port and her bow was secured. A rope tied over the capstan came loose and the ship was dragged onto her side on the beach. The captain tried to put her back in deep water but the propeller crashed against the rocks, leaving the ship to the mercy of the wind and waves. She was destroyed and they nearly lost the landing stage as well.

There is no doubt that a strong sense of community was soon established in the Nant, even though the work was hard and the people came from many different places. For instance, Professor Jones and Elen Rhys relate how Dr Huw T. Edwards, the Labour union leader, knew much about the early history of the village because his father had moved there from Penmaenmawr as a young quarryman and had rented one of the new houses with his wife. However, one day he had a bad accident in the quarry that kept him out of work for nine months. He had been working on a rope on the surface of the rock when suddenly the rock slipped and he fell with it and was very badly injured. In those days there were no sick schemes, so if you did not work, you did not get paid. Apparently, during the time he was incapacitated, on every second Saturday the Irishmen at the village would make a collection and bring a full wage to his household. The workers at the quarry were only paid every second Saturday, and with their wages they would first have to settle their account at the shop and pay their rent. Dr Huw T. Edwards told how in later life he would go for a walk through the village of Llithfaen so he could look down on the village of Nant Gwrtheyrn and raise his cap to those "warm-hearted Irish people."

Around 1900, the quarry manager was a Welshman from Conwy called Edward Jones who held the job for a quarter of a century, retiring in 1906. Although he initially lived in the Plas, when Ty Hen Farm became available he took it and while he was still the quarry manager he began to keep chickens and bees, and would sell his produce to the villagers. One of his workers was a lady called Elen Evans who came to work for him as a maid, but she soon also found herself milking the cows both morning and night in order to sell the milk to the quarry families. Elen got so fed up with the job after the manager's wife returned from a weekend in England and complained that the staff were not working hard enough, that she made the decision to join her husband in Red Granite, Wisconsin, where he had been working as a setter. The couple returned from the United States on the *Lucitania* in 1914, a year before the ship sank, and their descendants still live in the village of Llithfaen today.

When the Barics were first built, especially before any wives arrived, the quiet rural calm of the Nant became a rougher sort of place. One local historian called it "ungodly and uncivilised," claiming that the workers spent all their spare time "feasting and drinking." Elen Rhys and Professor Jones point out, however, that this historian was a staunch Welsh chapel-goer who disapproved of any non-religious pastime, especially drinking, so perhaps things were not quite as bad as this description might suggest. But in time, as women and children began to live in the village, a wooden building was built which was used as both a school and a chapel. It was called Y Babell Goed, which means the Wooden Pavilion. Initially, the Reverend David Evan Davies would come down to the village from Llithfaen to help out and do missionary work, while a Catholic priest would visit every second Monday. Then, in 1875, Nant Gwrtheyrn became a sectarian church belonging to the

Calvinistic Methodists. After the building of the new houses and the enlargement of the settlement a permanent chapel was built called Capel Seilo. It cost £3,000 and had enough seating for 130 people. Services were held in both Welsh and English, and Capel Seilo still stands today, although the old Babell Goed was destroyed in a storm.

By 1900, around 40 people were regularly attending Capel Seilo, and although the Nant was entitled to its own minister, none seemed very keen to remain in the position for long. The minister also doubled up as the schoolteacher – even though they had no particular training as such. So although a daily school was held in one of the houses at Mountain View, it only provided the children with a very basic form of education. This school was privately funded and run by the quarry company and when the village was between ministers, children had the choice of either climbing the old track to attend school in Llithfaen or simply staying at home. At times there was also a Sunday school held by the Capel Seilo minister, which was known to be attended by around 60 children.

In 1908, Caernarfonshire Education Committee took charge of the school and tried to improve the standard of education. But this was no easy task due to the fact that both teachers and children were frequently changing. The school inspectors were extremely unhappy about the situation, and one of them, Lewis Jones Roberts, made a suggestion in 1910 that the Education Committee accepted that the name of the school should be changed "from the hybrid Port Nant into the suggestive Nant Gwrtheyrn."

For those who did not wish to spend their spare time engaged in religious pursuits there was very little in the way of entertainment. There was never a public house in the village and early workers would visit the Victoria Tavern in Llithfaen. The track to this neighbouring village was steep and rough, and some workers were known to roll barrels of alcohol down it for consumption at the Barics. There were many stories about the drunken exploits of villagers as they negotiated the rough track between the two settlements. One spot along the route called Butler's Bend or Troad Butler, marks the spot where a lady called Mrs Butler died one night having got drunk in Llithfaen, and then frozen to death after presumably collapsing on the way home. At another place a small hawthorn tree was called Barlow's Bogeyman or Bwgan Barlow. Apparently an Englishman called Barlow was walking home late to the Nant one night after drinking a few pints when suddenly he saw the dark figure of a man blocking his way. He stopped in his tracks and when the figure seemed to move he turned on his heels and fled back to Llithfaen where he knocked on the door of the first house he came to. After Barlow had calmed down, two men went down with him into the Nant to investigate. After reaching the same spot, Barlow again stopped in his tracks. The ghostly figure was still there, but the two men quickly realised that all he had seen was a small hawthorn tree.

The busiest and most prosperous period enjoyed by the village was during the latter half of the nineteenth century. But by the end of the First World War the Porth y Nant Quarry had closed, and the number of schoolchildren had dwindled to around 17. Some of the men found alternative work in either the Cae'r Nant Quarry or the Carreg y Llam Quarry, but many others moved completely away from the village. Gradually, as Mountain View and Sea View were vacated, the people living at the old Barics moved into them. This proved to be fortuitous because in 1925 there was a landslide and some of the Barics fell into the sea.

During the 1930s there was a renewed demand for granite, which was needed for building new roads and tunnels. So for a short period another company reopened the Porth y Nant Quarry. This also brought new life to the school and chapel. But it was only short lived, as the prosperity enjoyed before the war had disappeared forever. By this time, the people who still lived in Nant Gwrtheyrn were beginning to feel more and more isolated from the modern world, and there was growing pressure for them to move to Llithfaen where they would have access to better facilities, such as shops, a doctor, and a secondary school. When the Second World War began the quarry closed for the final time and one by one the remaining families left. The 23 July 1948 edition of *Y Cymro* featured two photographs of people leaving the village. One of these was Mr John Roberts, who was pictured with his niece leaving their house in the Nant to live in Llithfaen. The second picture was of two men packing the school's furniture on a sledge, so that they could transport it up the unsurfaced 1-in-3 corkscrew hill. Two or three families of squatters moved into the empty houses in 1949 and the Education Committee reopened the school for a few years. But the days of a quarry community in the Nant were over and the last known people to leave did so 10 years later in 1959.

In 1970, Dr Carl Clowes moved to the area with his family to run the single-handed dispensing practice in nearby Llanaelhaearn.

Although his mother was Welsh-speaking, Dr Clowes was brought up in Manchester and learnt Welsh as an adult. He was determined to bring his children up as Welsh-speakers. The community was in immediate trouble however; there were rumours that the adjacent and last quarry at Trefor was going to close. Some 2,000 men had been employed in the quarries of Bro'r Eifl in the early part of the twentieth century. Llanaelhaearn school was in danger of closing because it was perceived to be too small and the number of shops in the village had fallen from seven to one. The Census return of 1971 showed a fall of one third in the parish population from the levels of 1921; concerted action was required if the downward trend was to be reversed and they were to avoid a similar fate to that of Nant Gwrtheyrn.

The new doctor led a successful campaign for the village school and then chaired the community movement that established Antur Aelhaearn, the first 'community cooperative' in the United Kingdom. This was an attempt to revitalise the area. They built their own factory, established training workshops, secured new housing in the village and established an Eisteddfod for the first time in half a century. Confidence was restored and there was a new sense of purpose in the community. Buoyed by the success at Llanaelhaearn, Dr Clowes then turned his attention to Nant Gwrtheyrn. Described by the casual visitor as a 'ghost village', he saw it as an important asset which could benefit the area. But how? During this period there was an increasing interest in the Welsh language, stimulated predominantly by the Welsh Language Act of 1967 and more people were interested in learning Welsh. There were many classes held throughout Wales and summer schools had been organised, the first being held in Harlech as long ago as 1961. Public bodies were, however, struggling to meet the bilingual requirements of the Act as those with the necessary professional qualifications were frequently found wanting in terms of their linguistic competencies – so important when large tracts of many regions in Wales were predominantly Welsh-speaking. Could the needs of employment for the area and a 'machine' to promote the language come together in some way? So the idea of a 'national language centre' was born with the doctor as the first Chair of Ymddiriedolaeth Nant Gwrtheyrn, a Trust he established with acknowledged tutors and friends in support.

There were many storms ahead. As the ideas for the Nant became public, so other interested parties came forward in com-

*Protest of villagers against threat to close the school in
Llanaelhaearn, sometime between March and July 1972*

Photograph courtesy of Dr Carl Iwan Clowes

petition, some 106 in total and not all acceptable: a place for the rehabilitation of offenders, a valley to hide oil tanks from the adjacent developing fields of the Celtic Sea, a centre for the rehabilitation of drug abusers and so on. Ymddiriedolaeth Nant Gwrtheyrn had no financial resources at their immediate disposal – only commitment and enthusiasm. This was used to good effect to outstrip the competition, lobbying at every opportunity, organising petitions and so forth.

By 1978, the process of attrition was complete and the Trust was able to buy the village from the Amey Roadstone Corporation under a mortgage arrangement for £25,000. They began to renovate the houses using Manpower Services Commission work programmes for the unemployed and, in April 1982, the first group of scholars arrived at the Nant, despite the fact that there were still no phones or electricity and only a noisy diesel generator for power! Further work on the remaining houses followed with learners groups, local authorities, private and voluntary sectors all contributing financially to secure the future. It has become truly a Centre for the people promoted by the people and, to date, some £1.5 million has been spent on restoring the village for those learning the language, which also has an impressive interpretive centre based on Capel Seilo together with Caffi Meinir – a warm and friendly focal point of sustenance for the weary scholar and casual visitor alike.

To date, some 25,000 individuals from 27 countries have been introduced to the Welsh culture and language at Nant Gwrtheyrn and the Centre has a renowned programme of courses for all stages of understanding, from the 'taster' to the 'advanced'. Many external bodies, including Acen itself, have also been holding courses at Nant Gwrtheyrn since 1989.

The Trust now owns 180 acres of Heritage Coast with several Special Sites of Scientific Interest. The whole village has been designated as Grade II by the Welsh heritage body Cadw and the Trust has gained accolades from *The Times,* Shell and the Royal Institute of British Architects for its contribution to the environment, bringing together as it does the physical, cultural and economic environments in one holistic programme.

14

SLIDING
FORTUNES

Oliver Frederick Evans was born in 1929 in the village of Penybanc, and it was there that he spent his early life. He was one of four children, the others being Albert, Roy and Winnie. For Oliver, despite the poverty that existed at the time, it was a very special place, with a strong sense of community. Penybanc consisted of around 20 cottages, mainly built in two rows, called Chapel Row and Stoney Houses. There were also three farms – Penybanc Farm, Cwmllwydrew Farm, and Pentwyn Farm – as well as a school, hotel and chapel.

On maps dating from the early nineteenth century, the cluster of buildings on this site are marked as Brithdir, and Penybanc historian Ifor Coggan explains that Cefn Brithdir was the name of the eastern ridge of the valley. The western ridge is called Cefn Gelligaer and relates to common grazing ground. The word 'Cefn' means 'back' as in the human back, but when put with another word like 'cefn gwlad', which literally means 'back country', this translates as 'countryside'. On this ridge was the Brithdir Level coal mine, which provided much employment for the area. At this time only the farm bore the name of Penybanc. There was also a workers cottage, called Ty Mawr, within the farm's top field.

Penybanc was located halfway between the villages of Fochriw and Deri in the county of Glamorgan, at the northern end of what is today the Cwm Darren Park, near Merthyr Tydfil. In fact, the Cwm Darren visitor centre is situated on the site of what had been Cwmllwydrew Farm, which translates as 'valley of the hoar-frost'. Part of the village had once been an isolation hospital, where contagious diseases were treated. At the time diseases such as smallpox were still common in Britain, especially in the more

A marquetry picture done of Penybanc by Ernest Gillard who lived at Number 10 Stoney Houses. It is a coffee table with his family tree underneath

Photograph courtesy of Edna Davies

A very rare photograph of Penybanc. Date unknown, but the lady who provided it lived there between 1932 and 1947

Photograph courtesy of Jean Lawrence

impoverished areas, so isolation centres existed all around the country. If a person contracted one of these illnesses they would go to live at the centre until they were well enough to return home. It goes without saying, of course, that some never returned. As Britain became slowly free of contagious diseases, such establishments were no longer needed.

If you examine a picture or map of the village you will see that it was built on the side of a hill above a valley. The hospital itself was situated in the lower part of the village, while the staff accommodation was in the upper part of the complex. When its closure was announced the whole site proved ideal for conversion into around 20 cottages to house workers for the area's expanding coal mining industry. It is believed that Penybanc Hotel was built as a lodging house for people visiting their relatives in the hospital.

Each of the cottages had two rooms downstairs and two above, joined by a twisting narrow stone staircase. They also had a lean-to at the back, which was a combined scullery and coal shed. In here would be kept mother's washing paraphernalia: the mangle, washing buckets, and flat irons, and the copper if they had one. Each cottage also had a small garden at the very bottom of which was a little stone shed. This was the toilet and although they followed the same pattern as other villages in having a shelf with a hole smartly cut in the centre, they differed by being connected to a main sewer by pipe. However, they did not have flushes and had to be flushed by means of a large bucket of water especially carried down to the bottom of the garden for this purpose. In Penybanc, these sheds were known as the 'Ty bach', or 'small house', and some were shared by two households.

Initially there was no piped water into the cottages at all, although it did eventually arrive. So in the early days water came via a communal standpipe, which was out in the street at the front of the cottages. There was no electricity in the village either, so lighting was provided in the main rooms by paraffin lamps and candles would light the journey up the twisting stairs to bed. Another candle was kept in a glass jam pot by the back door, which had a piece of string attached to it, enabling it to be carried to the small house during the night or during the dark winter evenings. But in time, each house was connected with electricity and provided with a meter into which a shilling could be slotted. Each dwelling was installed with two lights – one in the main downstairs living room and another in the master bedroom – for which a supply of shillings had to be constantly stocked, ready for when the meter ran out. However, the jam pot was still necessary when visiting the Ty bach at night.

The house was heated by a large brick-built fireplace, which had to be cleared out and relit every morning. Its shining black brickwork was cleaned by a cloth dipped in a material called black lead. This fireplace was in the main living room, but it was also here that all the cooking was carried out. For this purpose, a cast iron oven was positioned on one side of the fireplace. A large iron kettle was kept on the hob to provide hot water, and a three-foot long toasting fork hung on a nail at the side. The toast was made by placing the bread on a series of thick iron bars above the fire. The room was protected from sparks and falling pieces of burning coal by an iron fender standing on a stone hearth at the front of the fire.

Each day the ashes and any household refuse were carried out to a large cast iron container at the front of the street. This was called 'The Bin', and twice a week a man with a horse and cart would come to empty it out. During the hot summer months the smell could get very unpleasant.

When the railway line was built between Newport and Brecon it cut straight through the middle of the village, with half the cottages on the above slope and half below. However, it was not deemed necessary to build a halt at Penybanc itself, so if anyone wanted to catch the train they would have to walk to either Deri of Fochriw, both of which were about a mile and a half away.

Even though Penybanc had a hotel, school, and chapel, there was no telephone in the village and if there was an emergency or if the doctor was needed, this would also entail a walk to Fochriw to use the telephone there. "We did have the means of calling the fire service," explained Oliver Evans, "and this could be done by means of a red box on a pillar near Penybanc Hotel. In the box was a handle, which could be pulled after smashing a small glass window. This sent a signal by wire to the fire station at Bargoed."

After the handle had been pulled, an alarm would sound at the fire station and the number of the box that had been activated would be punched out on a piece of paper tape. The fire engine would then be sent on its way. "Our number was 144," stated Mr Evans, but as far as he remembered the box was never needed. Ifor Coggan, on the other hand, recalls that the box was only used "on the occassions when we, as mischievous lads, used to set it off for a dare."

Mrs Jean Lawrence, who lived in Penybanc from 1932 until she was married in 1947, remembers that a lady called Mrs Morgan would sell a few items, such as sweets and cigarettes, from the window of her cottage. She also points out that, unlike many traditional rural villages, there was no public house. No doubt miners would pick up their cigarettes from her window each day on their journey to or from work.

During the 1950s there were two shops in Penybanc, one of which being a grocery shop run by Ifor Coggan's grandfather Arthur Coggan from a shed in his garden in Chapel Row. The other was run by his uncle Vernon Coggan, who sold confectionary from his house in Stoney Houses. For other requirements, people either had to walk to Fochriw or get to the larger town of Bargoed. Other than that, the village was serviced by a series of tradesmen who visited on a weekly basis.

"A baker visited twice a week travelling from Bargoed," explained Oliver Evans, "and we gave him the nickname 'Gilbert stale cakes'. His bread was delicious but his cakes were not very good. It would occasionally happen that he would be unable to deliver his bread due to the road being blocked by winter snow. If this happened, he would put his bread delivery for the whole village into flour sacks and take them to the railway station at Deri where he would catch the train to Fochriw, throwing out the sacks of bread as the train passed through Penybanc. He never let us down! Other groceries were supplied from a shop in Fochriw (Morgan Harris) and each household had a 'standing order', which was delivered every Friday."

Milk was delivered by a lady called Maggie, who did a milk round on her horse and cart from Cwmllwydrew Farm. The untreated milk came straight from the herd and was ladled from Maggie's churn into the jugs as she arrived at each cottage. The milk had a thick layer of cream on top, which the people of Penybanc would skim off and put into a large glass jar with a screw top. By shaking the jar for about 10 minutes, the cream turned into a lump of pure delicious butter.

Coal was also delivered by horse and cart and then tipped outside the front door. It was then carried through the house in buckets to the coalhouse at the back. Transporting a tonne of coal in buckets was a time-consuming affair, as well as being very dirty. But the coal was essential for cooking and heating and most households included a miner, so it was supplied at a very reasonable rate.

Another weekly visitor by horse and cart was the haberdasher from Twynyrodyn near Merthyr Tydfil, called 'Danny the oilman'. He kept the village supplied with things like cleaning materials, candles, and paraffin for their lamps. Any item that he did not have on his cart could be ordered, and he would deliver them the following week. Similarly, clothes and shoes were supplied by 'Danny the packman', who would travel door-to-door with two suitcases. Again, orders could be placed with Danny and he would bring the garments on a subsequent visit.

Most of the cottages, if not all, were owned by an ex-school teacher also named Mr Evans, who I believe was no relation to Oliver Evans. He now owned and ran the main farm in the area, Penybanc Farm, with its large flock of sheep. These were allowed to freely roam the hillside above the valley, and were tended by shepherd Jack Lloyd and his sheepdogs.

"It was magic to watch him controlling these dogs as they rounded up the sheep," remembers Mr Evans. "Each dog responding individually to his commands. This puzzled me greatly and I asked him one day how he was able to control the dogs in this way. 'Well boy' he said 'I whistle in English to one and whistle in Welsh to the other' so the mystery was solved – or was it."

Overlooking the village was the reason for its continued existence, the Brithdir Level coal mine. Here as a boy, Oliver would sit for many hours watching the horses that were cloaked in steam created by their sweat, as they pulled the drams of shining black coal out of the mine entrance. A smithy was strategically placed near the mine entrance, from where the blacksmith could shod the horses or make the tools that were needed to dig out the coal.

"It was fascinating to watch the blacksmith at work, shaping a lump of red-hot metal into horses shoes and various other things," he says. "We were occasionally allowed to operate the huge bellows made of wood and leather, which powered his forge. We were then chastised by our parents for getting into such a dirty state when we got home. There was a stable there for housing the horses (later to become a bungalow) and a huge pile of steaming smelly manure outside, of which the people of the village could avail themselves for the vegetable garden."

The coal was transported by tramway along the hillside to Pentwyn, a nearby settlement, where it was loaded into railway wagons weighed on the weighbridge near Carmel Chapel and there despatched to its customers. Most men in the village, including

Mr Arthur Coggan of Penybanc delivering fruit and vegetables around the village of Fochriw in 1951, with his grandson Phillip sitting on the horse

Photograph courtesy of Ifor Coggan

Oliver's father, worked in the coal mining industry, either at Brithdir or at the Ogilvie Colliery on the other side of the valley.

Ifor Coggan's grandparents, as well as two uncles and six cousins, all lived in Penybanc, so he spent much of his childhood there and consequently has done a lot of research into the village. Concerning mining in the area he states:

> *The mining activity around the village (Fochriw) was intense and also comprised a number of 'levels' which were located on the eastern side of the valley just below the village and evidence of the tramways may still be observed between the conifers in the plantation. This network extended to the site of the Brithdir Level opposite Penybanc and converged at a junction adjacent to the river. It then travelled over a brick arched bridge, which is still in existence, and continued up a very steep gradient to Pentwyn via a steam-powered rope haulage. This building also survives and is located just below the crossroad junction at Pentwyn.*

The Brithdir Colliery was owned by the Dowlais Iron Company and managed by Mr J. Bevan. It employed 75 men underground and another 17 on the surface, and by 1876 was producing around 67,000 tonnes of bituminous coal a year, which was mainly sold for use as house coal. In 1861, it was recorded that the youngest miner in the Fochriw area was nine years old; the oldest being 71.

At this time, the miners generally tended to work at night in order to enjoy at least some daylight. A normal shift would start at midnight and end at around eight or nine the following morning, earlier on a Saturday. Their wages would have been around two shillings and eleven pence a day, which is roughly 15 pence in today's money. The Brithdir Levels ceased to operate in September 1938, which was a huge blow to the area's workforce – not only Penybanc but also for Fochriw itself. The Fochriw collieries had closed in 1924, so many miners from this once prosperous village had chosen to work in the Brithdir Level coal mine. This meant that by the 1940s the Ogilvie Colliery was the main source of employment for several mining communities.

Penybanc school was attended by the children of both Penybanc and Pentwyn, and there was great rivalry between the two groups. There were normally between 70 and 80 children enrolled in the school, which had two classrooms, with the very youngest in one and the remainder in the other. Each child had his own wooden desk, complete with a little inkwell at the top and a groove into which the ink pen was rested. The desk also had a lid that lifted up so that books and other things could be stored inside. The desk at which Oliver sat had formerly been occupied by his own father. He discovered this after lifting the lid and finding his initials carved on the inside. Sometimes the children also worked with chalk on slates that were positioned around the walls of the classroom.

Discipline at Penybanc school was severe and any misdemeanour was punished by the head teacher with a cane. He would use this across the fingers of a naughty child to inflict a stinging pain, and it was always kept on show as a constant warning of the punishment that would be dished out if any child were tempted to commit a misdemeanour.

Outside of school there was not much for children to do except roam the hills or play cricket and football. For cricket, odd bits of wood were used to make a bat and some stumps, and an inflated pig's bladder was used as a football. Other games recalled by Oliver Evans included 'kick the tin', 'pitch and toss' and 'bows and arrows'. But what the children did have was a swimming pool. On the railway line near Cwmllwydrew Farm was a large stone-built structure that had a huge cast iron tank on top of it. The tank was full of water and it was there to supply any passing steam locomotives that needed it. The children would climb up the side of this tower by means of an iron ladder, and then jump into the tank. It was much used by the village children during summer months.

All disagreements, explains Oliver Evans, "were settled by means of the Marquis of Queensbury's Rules and Tommy Sullivan's boxing gloves over three three-minute rounds. One bout in which I was engaged ended in a unanimous draw when I sustained a bleeding nose and my adversary a black eye."

The chapel played an important part in village life and children were expected to attend twice every Sunday, first for Sunday school and then for the evening service. The minister lived in Bedlinog and he would walk across the mountain come hail or shine to conduct the services. One highpoint of the year was the Sunday school's annual outing to the seaside, which would usually be to either Barry or Porthcawl. On that particular day, the village would be almost totally deserted and Mr Evans described how they would gorge themselves on candyfloss, lettered peppermint rock and pop. There were rides on the funfair and fun and games on the beach. It was a great day out and enjoyed by all. Ifor Coggan notes of Penybanc's Siloh chapel:

> *The chapel was probably built between 1871 and 1881 since there is no mention of it on the 1871 census but it is recorded in the 1881 returns. It was built by the Baptists probably with a view to cater for expansion in the population which never materialized. The chapel probably never had a resident minister and, from newspaper accounts during the early 1900s, pulpit duties were carried out by the ministers of Noddfa in Fochriw and Tabernacle in Deri, with Noddfa, Fochriw being responsible for the chapel.*

At that time, it appears that services were only held once a month with a Sunday school being held every week. From newspaper reports during the First World War, sermons were mainly in Welsh. A memorial service for the late Private W.J. Williams of Penybanc was held in August 1916; presumably he was killed on active service.

Not long after being built, the chapel had been closed again after running up debts of £800. But thanks to police sergeant Henry Williams of Fochriw, who was also a deacon of Noddfa, this debt was repaid over a period of some years and during the 1890s, with the help of his wife and son, he was responsible for restarting the Sunday school, with some 40 to 50 children in regular attendance. Over a period of 30 years Henry Williams was responsible for fundraising to the sum of about £3,000, and was presented with an illuminated address at Siloh Chapel by the East Glamorgan Baptist Association in January 1921.

"During the first 50 years of its life," continues Ifor Coggan, "the chapel hosted quite a number of special services, teas and concerts, this being all the more remarkable when it is realised that there was no public transport available and although the railway was open and passed through the middle of the village, there was no station at Penybanc. Anyone knowing the topography of the land between Fochriw and Penybanc will appreciate the dedication of the congregation who had to walk there, a distance of just over a mile, both half miles of which culminated at 1,350 feet at Pentwyn from a start of 1,110 at Fochriw and 900 at Penybanc."

It is thought that during the Second World War, probably during 1942, the chapel was sold to the Pentecostal Assemblies of God, the first mention of this being a report in the *Merthyr Express* during

January 1944 of a tea with the pastor William Griffiths of Bedlinog being the incumbent. He eventually moved to live in 2 Chapel Row, Penybanc. So Pastor Griffiths would have been the minister that Oliver Evans recalls walking across the mountains from Bedlinog, by which time services were being held weekly.

Oliver Evan's father, although a miner, did not work at the Brithdir workings above the village, but at the nearby Ogilvie colliery. "What a harsh job that was," he notes, and then goes on to describe how he would often spend all day, hewing coal from a seam that was often no more than only two feet six inches from floor to roof:

> *He would come home after his shift black with coal dust from head to foot absolutely exhausted and would sometimes sit at the table and fall asleep with his knife and fork in his hands. There were no pit head baths in those days and he had to bath at home. We had for this purpose a large beer barrel, which had been sawn in half and was filled with hot water from a bucket, which had been heated, on our coal fire. As he washed, the abrasions became visible, some of them on his back tattooed by the coal dust.*

In Oliver's early days, bath night for the village children was always on Friday, when the bath tub was dragged into the living room and filled with hot water in front of the roaring fire. Oliver's mother would then proceed to scrub him from head to foot. In due course, they built a large shed in the garden, which had a coal fired stove inside it. This, among other things, became the bathroom, and although going out to the shed on Friday evenings in the winter must have been pretty chilly, at least it stopped the mess and damp associated with bathing by the fire. Albert, Oliver's brother, recalls that the bath used by the four children had come from Brecon Army barracks where it had previously been used in the process of peeling and preparing spuds for the soldiers.

Every Monday their mother would wash the clothes. She would be in the shed all day with a rubbing board and green soap, washing her husband's filthy black working clothes last.

Oliver would have been 10 years old when the Second World War started in 1939, and he remembered hearing the announcement on a radio owned by Mr Penrose, who lived at No 1 Stoney Houses. Like most children he was terrified of what might happen.

The first thing to occur was the visit of an official gentleman who issued everybody with identity cards. Oliver was only a child, but he still had his own identity number: xJJ1.81.2. Then the rationing began and they were issued with ration books. But although some things were rationed, such as clothes and sweets, other things like potatoes and other vegetables were not. As most people in the village already grew much of their food, they managed reasonably well under the circumstances.

"The government encouraged everyone to produce as much food as possible," he explains, "to supplement the food ration and to this purpose most households produced vegetables in their own gardens. Keeping chickens became popular in the village because of the eggs and the occasional roast chicken for Sunday lunch. We had ducks, which Mam looked after, and they became our pets. I kept rabbits, which provided us with an occasional rabbit stew."

Because of the area's industrial base, it did not take long for the air raid siren to sound. For this purpose he recalls the colliery 'hooter' sounding intermittent blasts for a raid and a continuous blast for an all clear. When Cardiff was bombed, the people of Penybanc would see the sky lit red by the fires of burning buildings, but the village itself came through unscathed. The nearest it came to being bombed was when one aircraft jettisoned some bombs near Cwm Bargoed, but causing little damage. Had the Germans known that No 219 Fuel Depot (POL) manned by the Royal Army Service Corps had been created at the site of the old Fochriw Colliery, then their neighbours up the railway line might have come in for some unwanted attention, which could have proved devastating. A small Army detachment with a searchlight and gun pit was posted in a field below Penybanc school, but Mr Evans does not believe its gun was ever fired in anger. Jean Lawrence also remembers the Army camp because every Thursday the mobile library would come to the school to bring books for the soldiers to read.

A Home Guard platoon was established at Fochriw, which Oliver's father 'had' to join, as did all the other eligible men in the village. Before being known as the Home Guard, they were known as the Local Defence Volunteers and their uniform was little more than an armband emblazoned with the letters LDV. Thus attired, they would spend their evenings charging about the hills, searching for imaginary enemy parachutists, which Oliver described as "hilarious" to watch. But in time, the men of the Fochriw platoon were issued with proper uniforms and rifles, and Oliver was given the job of cleaning this each week before his father went on parade: whether he had access to any ammunition remains uncertain.

Like their parents, all school children were issued with "foul-smelling rubber gas masks," as a precaution against air attack employing poisoned gases that were seriously feared at the time. The gas mask was stored in a cardboard box and had to be carried everywhere by means of a piece of string that was attached to it. If a child arrived at school without it he would be sent home again to fetch it.

For Oliver, the war coincided with having to sit the eleven plus examination, which all children had to take at that time to determine the type of school they would attend thereafter. Oliver was fortunate enough to pass sufficiently high to secure a place at Bargoed Grammar School, where he spent the next "four happy years." The only drawback was the journey, which entailed walking the one and a half miles to Fochriw to catch a train to Bargoed, before another mile jaunt from the station to the school – all the time weighed down by a heavy bag of books and the "infernal gas mask." However, the return journey was made a little easier by following the example of Gilbert Stale Cakes. As the train passed through Penybanc, Oliver – and no doubt any other children with the same problem – would throw out their bag of books and retrieve it once they got back to the village.

"We were given a great deal of homework to do," he ponders, "and this occupied most of my evenings. It was difficult to study at home and during the summer months I would take my books to a quiet spot near the river, there to wrestle with the intricacies of physics and mathematics."

As well as working hard at his studies, Oliver played rugby for the school team on Saturdays. He, and I am sure his parents, were determined that he should get a good job and not have to follow his father into the colliery. His efforts paid off and after leaving school he found emloyment with British Telecom (BT), remaining with them for 40 years until his retirement. His son Raymond explains that: "Dad was a General Post Office engineer and stayed when it became British Telecom. His job was tracing and rectifying radio and television interference, which he loved, as it was very public related. He also built telephone exchanges in collieries and towns. When the GPO changed to British Telecom he became part of a team tracing the signals of illegal citizens band radios (CBs) and often had to go to court. Then he was one of only two engineers in Wales trained to operate television detector vans. There were only two of these vans in the beginning so Dad worked 80 to 90 hours a week."

Oliver left Penybanc when he got married, but his parents remained in the village until his father's health gave out and he was forced to give up his job and move to a modern house at Fochriw. A few years later his father died from the effect of the coal dust, which he had inhaled all his working life. His mother was never happy living in Fochriw and in due course moved back to Penybanc with an elderly aunt.

One evening in 1964 his mother was in bed when she was startled by a loud rumbling noise as the house began to shake. Part of the ceiling fell on to her bed and large cracks began to appear in the structure of the house. The entire village had been affected and the houses were subsequently rendered uninhabitable. "This was the death knell of Penybanc," he states, and all of its residents had to be re-housed by the local council.

His mother moved to a council flat at Gelligaer, as a close-knit, proud and independent Welsh mining community was irreparably broken up. It was with a heavy heart and indeed a tear in his eye, Oliver concluded, that one day shortly after this event he stood near the Penybanc Hotel to watch the demolition of the village.

Oliver Evans passed away in 2006, but certainly up until 2003 he would occasionally go back to Cwm Darren to where Penybanc stood to enjoy the tranquility of the place and to relive these and many other memories of his birthplace.

Edna Davies, who was also living at Penybanc at the time of the evacuation, was one of eight children, all born in the village, of which seven were girls and only one, the eldest, a boy. Her mother was a resident of the village, while her father came from Pantywaun, another of the area's villages destined to become lost. Edna was first cousin to Oliver Evans, who she refers to as 'Fred'. Edna's mother was the sister of Fred's father.

She recalls a happy, yet poor childhood, living at No 2 Stoney Houses. But when she and her husband Reginald got married in 1955, they moved into a flat under the chapel, which faced the railway line and had a fantastic view across the valley. "Sheer tranquility," she admits before explaining, "we lived there for seven years after our marriage, and then that dreaded earth tremor caused the village to close."

The couple moved to Fochriw, which Edna likens to "moving from Wales to England." By this time they were both Sunday school teachers and endeavoured to keep the chapel open as long as possible, so each week they would pick up children from Fochriw, Pentwyn and Deri to attend.

Reginald Davies came from Pentwyn, so naturally attended Penybanc school with the other children from his village. It was here that he first met Edna, and although he worked in the mines after leaving school, he hated it, so he eventually got a job working for Hoover in Merthyr Tydfil as a fork lift truck driver.

As teenagers they had both become members of Siloh. Edna was baptized at 13 and Reg at 14, at which time William Griffiths was still the pastor. The chapel played an important part in their lives, and as well as both being Sunday school teachers, Reg became a Chapel elder. The flat had belonged to the Morgan family, who had lived there before buying a farm in 1954. Edna was friendly with their daughter-in-law Margaret, and as her engagement coincided with the Morgans moving out, they were offered the chance to rent the flat for five shillings a week. They did so, and for the next seven years their rent did not increase.

Edna confirms that around 1900 the bottom four houses of the village were an isolation hospital. Her grandfather had the job of bringing patients to the hospital in a horse and cart. Her mother was born in September 1900, and as a girl (although living in the village) she was once a patient there herself. In later life she would tell her children how she would escape and run home after climbing out of the window. But a nurse would always be sent to take her back.

A little river flowed through the valley below the village, which today still meanders quietly through the Cwm Darren Park. As a girl she and her friends would go down to play at the bridge. There was a seat near the bridge which one of her friends called 'Edna's Seat'. Reg passed away in 1997 and Edna moved to be near her family. But on the occasion of her fiftieth wedding anniversary, 30 July 2005, she returned to walk from Fochriw to Deri along the old railway track, passing through Penybanc. She passed the rubble of the chapel where she stopped to say a prayer. She then passed the tree that had once stood in their garden, before continuing down to Edna's seat, where she sat and ate her lunch. Here she thanked God for his blessings to her and admits to shedding a few tears. Finally, she walked passed what had been Cwmllydrew Farm, and

Reg and Edna Davies in 1954 at Penybanc by the brook

Photograph courtesy of Edna Davies

on to Deri. Edna described Penybanc as being "the most beautiful place on earth," and admits that even now, with childhood and the village a distant memory, "it is still beautiful."

Earth tremors and subsidence in mining areas were nothing new, but one suggestion as to why Penybanc in particular suffered was due to the fact that the village sat over a large coal deposit. Although this was true, the village was safe due to an agreement made between the owners of Penybanc Farm, who not only owed much of the village but had a share of the mineral rights, and the owners of Ogilvie Colliery. They agreed that the coal would not be excavated for the very reason that it would destabilise the village. However, the son of Mr Evans explained that an ex-Ogilvie miner had once told his father that when the mine was due to close, they frantically "mined the shelf of coal away," which destabilized the ground and caused the subsidence. Penybanc Farm itself was eventually abandoned around 1970 when it was condemned following another earth tremor. Albert Evans suggests that the owners of the farm were part to blame for this situation themselves, hoping to gain from this final flourish of mining.

Pantywaun, the village from which Edna Davies' father originated, was demolished in 1962. At the time, this village near Dowlais, just a few miles north of Penybanc, was still inhabited by 80 people in 21 remaining houses. At its height, this little known village had around 50 homes, three pubs, three churches, a school, a railway halt, and a community hall. Earlier that year the residents, some who owned their properties but most as tenants, were served closing orders by Gelligaer Urban Council as all the houses were regarded as unfit for human habitation, and it would be far too expensive to repair the years of neglect.

The only property not served with such an order was the Royal Arms Hotel, which was owned by the Rhymney Brewery Company. However, even before the demolition of the rest of the village, its trade had been dwindling. The licensee, Mrs Elsie Evans, who lived at the hotel with her husband, Mr John Thomas Evans, told a *Merthyr Express* reporter at the time: "Our customers have drifted away and business has been on the slack side for weeks. During the past month, we have sold hardly any beer. Two or three men call occasionally for a few bottles, but that is all. On Saturday night, we had two customers, and from now on things will get worse." It was therefore inevitable that following the demolition of the village, the pub would eventually close.

The village itself was remote and isolated on top of an expanse of moorland above the Deri Valley. The local council may well have condemned the houses, but their decision was almost certainly driven in part by the fact that Taylor Woodrow wished to extend their opencast mining operations in the area. However, the people did not go without protesting. At a meeting between villagers and Gelligaer Urban Council, it was stated by the Clerk, Mr D. Morgan, that the houses were unfit for human habitation and incapable of being repaired at a reasonable expense. Mr Morgan said the residents of the village would be offered alternative accommodation, probably at the neighbouring village of Fochriw. One of the residents, Mrs Catharine Gallier, told the meeting: "We know the houses, in most cases, are not fit to live in. It's going to cost a lot to repair my house. I am a widow and I cannot afford the expense." The other residents said they were in the same position. The Clerk pointed out a provision under the Housing Act for compensation to be paid to an owner or a tenant where it was considered the property had been well maintained, and it seems that the people reluctantly applied.

Thus ended another of the area's mining communities, but Penybanc and Pantywaun were certainly not the first or last to vanish from the landscape of the Welsh valleys. For instance, another village in the Rhymney valley, Troedyrhiwfuwch (quite a mouthful), which translated as 'Foot of the cow's hill', was abandoned and demolished in the 1980s. A local man, David Lloyd Rees explains:

> It was situated on the main Rhymney to Bargoed road between the villages of Pontlottyn and New Tredegar. It consisted of a main street, which contained a post office, village shop, pub and farm. There were one or two other streets with a tin chapel and a school. The village was demolished because of subsidence and the danger of the homes sliding into the valley below. Today, the main road is still used. The farm is still standing, as is the post office and one house in one of the back streets, still standing in splendid isolation. Other than that, the whole village has been demolished.

15

THE CONCRETE
AND CLAY JUNGLE

Over the last 100 years, many parts of the countryside have seen changes as communities have been dissected by major road schemes, or been torn apart by the building of industrial parks and out-of-town shopping centres. For instance, people travelling into Cornwall during the summer only to find themselves sitting in a traffic jam for hours on the A38 trunk road near the infamous Dobwalls Hill, might have noticed the Moorswater Industrial Park just outside of Liskeard.

Today, Moorswater is famous for the wide range of businesses that are accommodated on the site, but not that long ago Moorswater was a thriving little village, the remnants of which can still be glimpsed through one or two cottages and houses dotted around this rural concrete jungle. As a village, Moorswater itself was initially all about canal barges, trains and a famous viaduct designed by Isambard Kingdom Brunel.

Derrel Weaver was born in Moorswater in 1954 and lived in a house appropriately named Railway View. He says: "our village was destroyed by the new by-pass that created the monster that is Dobwalls Hill in 1975."

Derrel describes Moorswater as having been "the epitome of the Cornish village." It had the Forge Café, which was also the village store. Then there was the chapel, the village institute and the playing fields. There were allotments for most of the villagers, a bus stop, and a red telephone box. It was certainly significant enough to have both a brass band and a football team, the latter of which won the Launceston & District KO Cup in 1937. In the same year, which was their best ever, they also won the Cornwall County League and the Liskeard and District League Shield. Moorswater

Taken about 1973 just as the General Post Office were clearing the old poles from their yard at Moorswater, some can still be seen. Looking back towards Derrel Weaver's house, Railway View, with the old chapel up behind to the right. All these buildings are now gone

Photograph courtesy of Derrel Weaver

football team were joint tenants of Lux Park with Liskeard Rugby Club, and after Liskeard Football Club was disbanded in 1935 due to mounting debts, the men from Moorswater kept football alive in the area until the Liskeard team were able to reform in 1946.

One thing the village did have which others did not were the steam engine sheds! Steam engines were constantly passing through the village causing great excitement for the local children. Derrel's father actually worked as a signalman at Coombe Junction signal box, and he remembers many enjoyable train rides.

The railway came to Moorswater because of its unique position. The Cornwall Railway, designed by Brunel, linked Plymouth with Falmouth. The section from Plymouth to Truro was opened on 4 May 1859, and along its route was a station at Liskeard. A few miles to the north, on the edge of Bodmin Moor around Caradon Hill, were the South and West Caradon mines where there was a rich vein of copper ore. And at the nearby Cheesewring Quarry at Minions, granite was being extracted. In order to transport this copper and granite down to the sea at the nearest port, which was the fishing harbour of Looe, The Liskeard and Caradon Railway was started in 1844 and opened in 1846.

The railway line, which was roughly eight and a half miles long, went from Caradon Hill down to Moorswater, just outside of Liskeard. Eventually the line was extended to the Cheesewring Quarry at Minions via a long incline at Goonamena. And in time there were further extensions, which included a track completely encircling Caradon Hill, enabling further pick up points.

At Moorswater, the ore and granite was loaded onto barges for the final leg of the journey along the Liskeard and Looe Canal, which had been opened in 1827. But before long the canal was unable to cope with the increasing traffic. So in 1860, the canal company opened its own railway link from Moorswater down to Looe. The railway was actually built on the bed of the redundant canal. Until 1862, when steam trains took over the task, the wagons carrying the ore would simply run down the track from the Caradon mines to Moorswater under their own momentum, but were hauled back up the laborious slope again by horses.

In 1901, this little branch line was linked to the main Great Western Railway system at Liskeard, via Coombe Junction, which is where Derrel's father would one day work. However, at Liskeard, the main line and the branch line were kept separate. Today, the train for Looe, which can still be taken by passengers and tourists, leaves Liskeard from a separate station, which is an old timber building at the side of the main station. From here the branch line curves beneath the great viaduct that carries the main line on towards Truro. At Coombe Junction passenger trains reverse direction to reach Looe, after the points have been operated by the train guard. This is one of the few places on the British railway network where passenger trains are still routinely switched in this way. However, the line still continues beyond Coombe to a cement terminal at Moorswater. After reversing at Coombe, the line travels close to the East Looe River, which opens out to become a tidal estuary. The part of the line linking Liskeard and Coombe Junction is renowned for being unusually steep, and drops around 200 feet.

In 1916, the line that ran down to Moorswater from Caradon Hill was closed. This was brought about by the closure of the ore mines around Bodmin Moor. In fact, a trip to the area around Cheesewring, close to the Hurlers Stone Circle on Bodmin Moor, will reveal the remains of quarry workers cottages. However, because Moorswater was now suitably connected to main line Britain, it maintained its railway link through the engine sheds and concrete works, as well as its connection to the little single track branch line running down to the coast. But in 1966 the Looe Valley Line found itself facing closure under Richard Beeching's Reshaping of Britain's Railways plan, although luckily the decision was reversed with only two weeks before its scheduled demise. Today, this scenic little line still runs between Liskeard and Looe, and as well as stopping at Coombe Junction, there are request stops at Saint Keyne, Causeland and Sandplace.

Among many achievements, Isambard Kingdom Brunel was known for building a series of timber viaducts to take the Great Western Railway through the West Country, although none survive to this day. But there are still many of his original stone piers that were built to support the wooden viaducts, which sometimes stand alongside replacement structures. One of the most notable examples of this can be found at Moorswater, where you can still see some of Brunel's original piers near the viaduct that now strides the Looe branch line.

Brunel's original viaduct was 147 feet high, 954 feet long and rested over 14 piers. It was replaced by the new stone viaduct with cast iron parapets in 1881. "Brunel's old viaduct towers are still there today," confirms Derrel. "The bridge section was wooden and was long gone by my childhood, but the ivy that climbed up the

Steam engine at Moorswater, just below the Weaver house in the late 1950s. Note the remains of Nissen huts piled up in the front

Photograph courtesy of Derrel Weaver

The last train out of Moorswater in 1961, towing clay trucks, just going under the viaduct. A young Derrel Weaver is wearing his dad's Chindit hat! This picture taken by his mum is probably the only picture anywhere of this event

Photograph courtesy of Derrel Weaver

towers was so thick, it was like a rope ladder and as kids we would climb right to the top of the towers!"

The biggest industry affecting the village during the early twentieth century were the ECLP (English Clays, Lovering and Pochin) china clay works. As a boy Derrel can remember steam trains, and later diesels, running clay trucks in and out of the works all day. Some times these trucks would be parked up over the weekend, which provided an opportunity for him and his friends, Mike Rickard and Geoff Newson, to raid them for "great hunks of clay." Many clay fights took place in the village of Moorswater. Today, there is still a cement terminal at Moorswater and cement trains still operate on the branch line out of what had once been the old Moorswater engine sheds. The old weighbridge for the railway trucks is also still evident and can be found just before the remains of the old station platform, although nothing of the station building itself remains. Incidentally, Geoff Newson's father was an AA patrolman, first being seen around the village with a motorbike and sidecar, before he was later issued with a mini van in the 1960s.

But as well as the railway and the clay works, Moorswater had a garage with an attached workshop. It also had a telegraph pole yard belonging to the General Post Office. This was another place at which the local children would find hours of amusement, where hundreds of poles were stacked on trellis racks. Mr Weaver describes how he and his friends would run over these stacks of racked poles, "and of course underneath them! We would play on them and make secret camps in the maze beneath."

Along the railway line there was a tall water tower for the use of passing steam engines. A wooden aqueduct went from the top of this tower, carrying water to the engine sheds. Mr Weaver does not claim that he and his friends used to swim in the tank, as Oliver Evans and his friends did at Penybanc, but they would certainly scale the tower and climb precariously along the wooden aqueduct to the roof of the engine sheds. "What fun!" he reflects, "real village life, all gone now except my mum's cottage and a half a dozen scattered houses, now surrounded by the road and industrial estate."

Derrel's mother, who was the very last of the original villagers to remain living in one of these houses, died in 2006, aged 90. He admits that before the arrival of the concrete, life was idyllic and everywhere you went, you were aware of the ever-present viaduct towering above you.

Derrel Weaver's mum Molly and her friend Silvia Lake, who is carrying Derrel's older sister Dawn. She was about two at the time, in 1948. Brunel's old pillars at Moorswater can be seen through the span of the viaduct. This view has little changed today

Photograph courtesy of Derrel Weaver

This close community of local Cornish families who had lived there for generations was effectively destroyed when the decision was taken to build a road through its heart, a road which today leads to nightmare tailbacks for miles every summer. A similar situation can be seen a little further along the road at Dobwalls where much more of the village still remains, although the trunk road ploughs straight through its centre creating a nightmare for the people who live there. Yet Derrel believes that today's insufferable traffic congestion could have been avoided, and the Moorswater community saved, if the project had been given better consideration in the first place.

Derrel suggests that the original road that existed at Dobwalls Hill worked well enough when it had just two lanes. "The traffic flowed up," he points out, "and the traffic flowed down. As soon as they tried to funnel two lanes into one at Dobwalls, the nightmare began. The villagers tried to tell them but no one would listen. Our fate had already been sealed by grey men in grey suits with grey hearts. I will always be bitter and angry, and now, all these years later, they are desperate to build a new bypass to ease the congestion that we predicted all those years ago in 1975."

One wealthy family in the area were the Crinks, who lived in a nearby mansion, and owned a brewery yard at Moorswater which provided further employment for the village. Mr Weaver explains that the brewery yard was "at the top of the village behind the bus stop." The Crinks' mansion is still in evidence, but the yard, bus stop and village were all destroyed by the bypass.

As well as his mother's house, which now stands behind a huge retaining wall, another surviving property was that of Mrs Stevens, in the garden of which were the remains of an old waterwheel and lime kiln. He points out, however, that although his mother's house remains, the bypass claimed their orchard. "An American jeep apparently came over the orchard wall one night during the war," he relates. Elements of the American 29th Division were camped all around the Looe and Liskeard area during the pre-invasion build up for D-Day, which included a camp at Moorswater.

He can also remember the British Army coming to Moorswater in the early 1960s on manoeuvres. Here, they practiced planting demolition charges on the old viaduct towers. They did this by drilling into them, but unfortunately one of their massive drill heads got stuck. It remains there to this day, and Derrel states that, "if you go and look down the railway line, go under the viaduct and immediately to your left is one of the old towers with the drill piece still stuck in it."

During the summer the Forge Café and village store was a popular spot for village people to meet and chat. It was owned by Mr and Mrs Daniels, and when in 1975 it was doomed for demolition, the Daniels invited everybody in the village to visit them and take away any item free of charge, so that they might remember it. Derrel took away a round brass coach mirror, which he still has.

He also remembers one or two of the other people who lived in Moorswater, as it was: "Mr and Mrs Coles lived under the viaduct. Stan was an engine driver and a miserable old git. He had an allotment behind the engine sheds and we would sneak in and go raspberry and goosegobbin! Mr and Mrs Bray lived below us and Dad would send me down at times to buy an ounce of A1 tobacco and a packet of green Rizla papers. Old Mr Bray, who was a porter up at Liskeard station, would disappear into a mysterious room and come out with the goods. It was always dark in that house and the only sound was the ticking of the clock."

Derrel's mother Molly was a local girl from Moorswater, but his father George first came to the village during the war, when he was stationed there with the Army after the evacuation of Dunkirk. The couple met locally, fell in love, and were married in 1941. Not long after that George disappeared again, this time to go and fight in the Burmese jungle for four years with the Chindits. When he eventually returned to Cornwall, the couple lived with Molly's mother Gladys, and had two children. George found employment with the railways, which is how he came to be working at Coombe Junction as a signalman.

Another type of Moorswater resident that Derrel remembers were the otters. Apparently, much of what is now the industrial estate was once a marshy wetland bordered by the village football field. No doubt the name 'Moorswater' derived from this situation, where water would have run down from Bodmin Moor in streams and rivers: just the sort of habitat that English Nature spend millions on today trying to protect. "There were otters there when I was a child," Derrel recalls with delight. "The swamp had dozens of big alder trees and if you climbed one and waited long enough you would occasionally see an otter."

Thirty years later, as Britain's traffic continues to increase, especially for Cornwall as more and more tourists and holiday-makers flood into this relatively small area throughout the year,

Inside Greensplat Methodist chapel, which was finally knocked down in 1997 due to the expansion of the china clay works and the need to divert a road. The girl in the front row, sixth from right, is Jeff Barry's mother Violet

Photograph courtesy of Lesley Morcom/Jeffery Barry

the Highways Agency are again making plans to improve the bottleneck that is faced by these and commercial vehicles at Dobwalls Hill. The problem with Dobwalls is that it is one of the few remaining stretches of the A38 that still has single lane traffic. The solution presumably would be to turn it into a dual carriageway: but at what cost?

Derrel Weaver noted that at Moorswater the ECLP china clay works were the biggest employer in the village. Travelling west from Moorswater to the Gover Valley near St Austell, you will arrive in china clay country proper, and a visit to the Wheal Martyn China Clay Heritage Centre will give you an insight into the people and industry of this area. Due to the success and expansion of the local china clay industry, rural homes were slowly lost and their ghostly remnants are strewn along the valley.

Lesley Morcom, who lives in Trewoon near St Austell, explains that within a few miles of her home there were several communities, all of which have now disappeared. The nearest was Goonamarth, which was roughly a mile from Trewoon. A mile to the west of that was the hamlet of Halviggan; two miles to the east was the larger village of Greensplat; and a few miles to the north was Karslake. "All this area has gone," she states, "because of ECLP, then ECC, and now Imerys."

Henry Davis Pochin (the P of ECLP) was an industrial chemist during the nineteenth century, later elected to Parliament as an MP for Stafford. He invented a process which used ammonium sulfate and alumina as a low cost alternative to alumstone in the production of alum cake, which was used for paper manufacturing. This process needed china clay, so he bought a number of china clay mines in Cornwall, the biggest of which was the Gothers drying works near Roche, a few miles to the north of St Austell.

At Gothers there were several large drying kilns, each of which had its own tramway. A fleet of steam locomotives, called Pochin's Puffing Billies, would carry the dried clay across Goss Moor to a loading wharf on the St Dennis Branch line. At the wharf, the clay would be transferred from the tramway's crude wagons to standard gauge wagons. For the return journey to Gothers, the tram wagons would be loaded with coal used for firing the kilns. Pochin's Puffing Billies were without brakes, so having reached the kilns they could only be stopped by jamming a piece of wood between the spokes of the wheels as the tram rolled down the gentle slope.

H.D. Pochin became one of the largest china clay producers in the country, another being Lovering. In 1932, English China Clays acquired both Lovering and H.D. Pochin, and formed ECLP. In due course, the families of both Lovering and Pochin sold their shares in the company and their names were dropped from the title. English China Clays (ECC) had four divisions: ECC construction materials, ECC quarries, ECC transportation, and ECC international. In 2000, the entire group was bought by Imetal SA, which more recently changed its name to Imerys.

Farming had been the main occupation of the people in the Gover Valley for hundreds of years, and the small village of Greensplat (sometimes spelt Greensplatt) mainly comprised of farms and farm labourers cottages, until the china clay works offered a new source of employment. At this time, some people made use of old disused railway wagons as accommodation. The village had both a Methodist chapel and an adjoining Sunday school, and the whole area was crossed by a network of footpaths regularly used by both workmen and children as they made their way to school at nearby Carthew.

In 1997, due to the expansion of the china clay works and the need to divert a road, the Methodist chapel at Greensplat was finally knocked down, which left one remaining cottage in the village named Kenwyn. Greensplat chapel was built in 1873 by the United Methodist Free Church, although the village had been included in the St Austell Wesleyan Preachers Circuit for cottage gatherings since the early 1850s. The chapel was later extended and by 1904 the list of chapel trustees give a good indication of how local employment relied on the clay mines, as the 13 individuals are noted as being two farmers, two enginemen, but nine clay labourers. The following description of the chapel is provided by the Historic Environment Service of Cornwall County Council:

The chapel was built in a simple gothic style; the front wall having a circular date plaque reading 'Greensplat MFC 1873' situated high in the gable, over three stepped lancet windows. A pair of gabled openings flanked the recessed central doorway. Near the base of the front wall were dressed foundation stones in the names of Philip Hooper (Carran Carrow) and Miss Marian Stoeker (Glen View, St Austell), placed here on August 11th 1896. The chapel consisted of rendered stone masonry walls beneath Dalabole slate roofing. Three lancet window openings containing replacement wooden frames and yellow coloured obscured glass were located in both the east and west walls of the chapel, probably added in the 1960s. The Sunday school had two simple stained glass windows in the east and west walls, with similar glazing used to light ancillary rooms. A porch providing access to the Sunday school had a sculpted render pyramidal roof and spherical finial. North of the Sunday School were a pair of green painted wooden double doors which lead into a separate store area.

There is no doubt that although some of these farming communities had existed for hundreds of years, by the turn of the twentieth century their numbers had swelled as a direct result of people coming into the area to work in the china clay industry. To compensate for this increase, the Sunday school attached to the chapel was enlarged in 1929.

Lesley Morcom was born in 1966: her father was born at Penisker Farm in 1936. She confirms that at the moment of writing one final house stands at Greensplat, which she describes as "quite a sizeable settlement complete with chapel and small holdings, some of which were converted railway carriages. Greensplat even had its own brass band." The one remaining house is boarded up and she believes that bats have moved in.

Of the other communities at the top of the Gover Valley, she believes that Karslake comprised of around 24 houses and Halviggan about 10, the last of which was knocked down in the 1990s. Most of Lesley's memories are associated with Goonamarth, which was not really a separate village but an outlying part of the Greensplat community, consisting of a row of eight cottages called Blackberry Row and several other individual houses.

"I can only remember a few houses, as some had already been knocked down," she explains. "The first to go was Blackberry Row in 1967. Mr Pethick's house went in the late 1970s, or early 1980s. Next to go was Mr Pentecost's, then Mini Kent's, then Higher Biscovillack Farm. The last place to go was Mr Sleeman's house, Goonamarth Farm, which was knocked down in September 2001. The only place left now is Penisker Farm." Penisker, she goes on to explain, was actually two farms attached to each other, only one of which now remains, the other being reduced to rubble.

Lesley recalls being told by an old neighbour, Mr Dyer, that a policeman had once been shot at Halviggan. An investigation into

Greensplat Junior Band, date unknown. The man holding the name tag is Len Manhire, who was Jeff Barry's uncle

Photograph courtesy of Lesley Morcom/Jeffery Barry

Blackberry Row, Goonamarth, where Jeffery Barry lived as a child. These houses were knocked down in 1967

Photograph courtesy of Lesley Morcom/Jeffery Barry

this incident reveals that it took place during a clay worker's strike in 1913, when the Worker's Union fought for better conditions and pay. On the evening of 22 September, a crowd of strikers attacked an engine house at Halviggan and one of them, Howard Vincent, shot police constable Collett in the leg.

Having discussed Halviggan with her mother, Lesley also explains that "in the late 1940s or early 1950s, a Mr Sid Trudgian shot his wife and then himself. Also in the 1950s, a Mr Willie Hore cut his throat and wrists, and a Mr Charlie Heard ate rat poison." Apparently the poison took so long to work that he shot himself as well. "Maybe it's a good job that the place is gone," she contemplates, and although we do not know the reasons why these individuals took their lives, perhaps they indicate the depression and stress that people in the area suffered at the time.

During the Second World War many Americans were stationed around Halviggan and their engineers were responsible for turning what had previously been the cart track to Goonamarth into a properly surfaced road. At the top of the Gover Valley is a place called Carnstents, where lived a lady the locals nicknamed 'Grassy Back', due to the fact that she was often seen at Halviggan while the Americans were there. She was certainly one of the local characters whose swearing, Lesley suggests, would make the youth of today blush. She was also known to break glass bottles in the lane outside of her home and pull tree branches across it, as she did not like people passing her cottage.

"If she was in St Austell and she knew you," continues Lesley, "she would walk out in front of your car, put her hand on the bonnet to stop you, climb in, and would not get out until you took her home. Many a time in town I would be grabbed and pulled down a side street by my mother and told 'quick Grassy Back is coming'."

The cottage in question and the one beside it were only put on mains water around 15 years ago. Before that their residents would have to go down the garden, over a footpath, and down a bank to where their water came from a pipe. Up until recently both cottages had no mains electricity either; one used a generator and the other was still being lit by tilly lamps. Lesley Morcom believes that Grassy Back's house, which was owned by the Trewithian Estate, has since been connected. After the old lady went into a home and subsequently died, the house was sold, whereas the cottage next door to it, which the Estate still owns, remains without mains electricity. She also notes that Penisker Farm, where her father was born, is also owned by the Trewithian Estate.

"When I was three years old," says Lesley, "I can remember going over the road with my granfer with yesterday's paper, to give to Mini Kent. She would be sitting at a large table, beside an old Cornish range wearing a pinny. That is my earliest memory of Goonamarth."

Jeffery Barry actually grew up in Greensplat, which in 1943 he says was "a thriving community centred on the Methodist chapel." He states that it was quite a "poor but very happy place to live."

"My childhood," he continues, "was a very happy one with vast areas of downs and moorland to play on. The 'downs', as we called it, were criss-crossed with literally miles of footpaths. With our little packed bags, a bunch of kids would set off and be gone all day on an adventure. The paths were also used by workmen to reach their place of work. School was also reached by footpaths through the woods and fields, passing by the big house of Lady Ivy Martyn, finally emerging at Carthew by the old post office."

Whilst still quite young, Mr Barry moved to Blackberry Row, Goonamarth, which he agrees was "still part of the same community." It was again served by numerous footpaths that led to Greensplat, Trewoon, and down through the Gover Valley to St Austell. "It comprised of eight houses made from a converted clay dry," he states. There were no mains facilities at all, not even water, which was collected from a chute or spring about 50 metres away. Each house had a rather large back garden with a stone built toilet at the top. These buildings had corrugated iron roofs, while inside was a pine seat with a bucket sized hole. Under the cover of darkness, the buckets were taken to the nearby River Gover where their contents were discharged, duly ending up on Pentewan beach. Oil lamps and candles were the only form of lighting and the houses burned coal and wood for warmth and cooking.

"Over the years," he concludes, "I have seen almost all of the area described disappear. It breaks my heart to see it happening and I have no doubt a lot of others feel the same way. The only link to my past remaining are the footpaths at the head of the Gover Valley leading from Blackberry Row through Higher Biscovillack and Goonamarth Farms."

Poignantly, Mr Barry points out that, other than this network of footpaths, there is little evidence left of the places where he spent

A bus waits in front of Goonamarth Drys. Jeff Barry believes it shows the annual village outing to the seaside, organised by the people of Blackberry Row. "With there being eight houses at Goonamarth," he says, "plus two farms and two cottages near the Dry, there would have been enough people to fill the coach." The lady to the right of the bus holding the baby could be Monica Wickett

Photograph courtesy of Lesley Morcom/Jeffery Barry

his formative years, stating that he is unable to show his grandson the places where he himself had played as a child.

Many homes in the Gover Valley have therefore been lost through the expansion of the china clay works, while other villages and hamlets all over Britain have been swallowed up by the expansion of the concrete jungle of industry, road development, or to become suburbs of major towns and cities.

During the course of the twentieth century there were many different reasons why villages, hamlets, or isolated homes were abandoned or lost, and many of the causes remain with us today. 'Ghost villages' are now part of the rural landscape of Britain and are a permanent reminder of how quickly community life – and its values – can disappear in our ever-changing and unpredictable world.

ACKNOWLEDGEMENTS

I would like to thank the following people for their help during the writing of this book: Anthony Power (director, Morwellham Quay); Dennis Corner; Gordon Hayes; Graham Haw; Roger Taylor (Somerset Archaeological and Natural History Society); Daniel Medley (general manager, Wookey Hole Caves); Ruth and Frank Milton; Steve Melia; Wilfred Login; Anne Morgan (archivist, Plymouth and West Devon Record Office); David and Cathryn Higham; Michael Pye; Alan Brown; Chris Wooler; Margaret Fulwell; Vivien Meath (editor, *Clitheroe Advertiser and Times*); Gareth Owen; John Shapland; Alan Plester; Paddy Apling; Mr R. Pitcher; Nancy Payne; Ken Mitchell; Doreen Charles; Terence Meaden; John Williams; Neil Skelton; Ruth Underwood; Rosalind Hooper; Major M.H. Burgess (range officer at the Armoured Fighting Vehicle Gunnery School, Lulworth Camp); William Hayter; Meg Kingston; Oliver Frederick Evans; Raymond Evans; Albert Evans; Ifor Coggan; Edna Davies; Jean Lawrence; David Lloyd-Rees; Jim O'Rourke; Derrel Weaver; Lesley Morcom; Rod Ohlsson; and Sharon MacCuish (Historic Environment Service for Cornwall County Council).

REFERENCES AND FURTHER READING

I would like to give particular thanks to Stephen Fisk, whose website (www.abandonedcommunities.co.uk) was an invaluable help while writing the sections on Dylife (pages 19–24), Myndd Epynt (pages 126–129), and St Kilda (pages 73–84). Stephen Fisk notes himself that sources for his own research include Michael Brown's book, *Dylife: An industrial and social history of a famous Welsh lead mine* (published by Y Lolfa, 2005).

Also thanks to Richard Muir for permitting quotes from his book, *The Lost Villages of Britain* (published by Michael Joseph Limited, 1982).

Much of the chapter on Mingulay (pages 38–46) is based on the research of Ben Buxton for a chapter in *The Decline and Fall of St Kilda* (published by the Islands Book Trust, 2005).

Thanks to Elen Rhys for permission to use her research on Nant Gwrtheyrn, and that of the late Professor Bedwyr Lewis Jones, published on the website of Cwmni Acen of Cardiff, the On-line Language Centre for Wales (see www.acen.co.uk). All courses held at Nant Gwrtheyrn can be found on the National Centre's website (see www.nantgwrtheyrn.org). I would also like to thank Dr Carl Iwan Clowes, the president of Nant Gwrtheyrn, for checking the article and updating it with his own account of Nant Gwrtheyrn's development since being purchased by the Trust in 1978.

Thanks to Jeffery Barry for letting me quote from his article, 'A personal loss', which was first published on the Gover Valley website (see beehive.thisiscornwall.co.uk, select 'local issues', and then 'Gover Valley').

Other sources of reference:

- *Hallsands: A village betrayed* by Steve Melia
  (Forest Publishing, 2002)
- *Sisters Against the Sea* by Ruth and Frank Milton
  (Devon Books, 2005)
- *The Guide Book and Trail Guide for Morwellham Quay*
  (Morwellham & Tamar Valley Trust, date unknown)
- *The Wookey Hole Caves* by Olive Hodgkinson
  (Wookey Hole Caves Ltd, date unknown)
- 'All tracks lead to Clicket Mill' by Hilary Binding
  (from the *West Somerset Free Press,* 2 February 2001)
- *With Nature and a Camera* by Richard Kearton
  (Cassell and Company, 1898)
- *Little Imber on the Down: Salisbury Plain's ghost village*
  by Rex Sawyer (The Hobnob Press, 2001)
- *A Short History of Tyneham* by Brian Leighton
  (Media Support Wing, HQ Armour Centre, Bovington, 1978)
- *My Life with RAF St Eval* by Roy Dunstan
  (publisher and date unknown)
- 'Poignant tale of a woman who fought for her land'
  by Keith Skipper (from the *Eastern Daily* Press, April 1999)
- 'The voice of an earthquake' by Gerald Searle
  (from the *Clitheroe Advertiser and Times,* July 2006)
- 'The Tyneham trail' leaflet by Julie Astin and Hugh Waller
  (produced by Paul Thorne Graphics, date unknown)
- Army Training Estate Public Information Leaflets
  for ATE Pembrokeshire and ATE East (date unknown)
- The Stonehouse Inn, Thruscross website, which contains a
  short history of West End (see www.stonehouseinn.co.uk)
- The Isle of Purbeck website (see www.isleofpurbeck.com)

INDEX